FAUST THE DANCING CAT
DOES VEGAS

By Signe A. Dayhoff, PhD

Faust the Dancing Cat Does Vegas
by Signe A. Dayhoff, PhD

Copyright ©2019 by Signe A. Dayhoff, PhD
Published by Effectiveness-Plus Publications LLC
80 Paseo de San Antonio
Placitas, New Mexico 87043-8735

Cover design by BDT/around86 @fiverr.com
Photo ©iStockPhoto/AmyDreves

ISBN: 978-0-9970168-9-5

DEDICATION

In Faust's first book, *What Faust the Dancing Cat Taught Me*, this gray skeletal feline contrives our initial meeting, manipulates me to become his constant companion, and then spends his time developing his talents as a dancer/acrobat when we aren't encountering wild-and-woolly adventures on dark, lonely roads or with "redneck" cops. In his second book, *Faust the Dancing Cat Tackles Strippers, Scammers and Bears*, he teaches college, increases his artistic repertoire, participates in breaking and entering for a loved one, and creates delightful chaos in a funeral home. In his third book he almost becomes a cable darling, controls coaching sessions, has "near-death experiences" in Death Valley, foils a sexual attack on his companion, and has his Big-Time audition.

This final book in the Faust the Dancing Cat trilogy is dedicated to Faust who helped me become more anxiety- and sabotage-free and more risk-taking. He also opened up for me the overwhelming joy of having a cat companion/alter ego.

Once again, it is dedicated to all companion-animal, no-kill rescue organizations locally, like Corrales, NM's C.A.R.M.A, nationally, and around the world, which work tirelessly for homeless animals to be adopted into loving homes.

It is also dedicated to all those who have enjoyed and praised Faust's antics in his first and second books and have clamored for more of his eccentric adventures.

TABLE OF CONTENTS

1

MARCHING ORDERS

I couldn't believe it. How could they be so inconsiderate! I had just received their notice. The owners of my rental on Willow Road in Sudbury, Massachusetts, were actually coming back to the States after years working abroad. In their proclamation letter they stated, of all things, they wanted their split-level home back! After all these years? I mean, there *must* be some statute of limitations that says if you've abandoned your house to someone else for x-number of years, the house no longer belongs to you after that time but to the person who has fought cat tooth-and-nail to keep it safe from slavering, marauding zombies and telemarketers.

Okay, so I didn't really believe that. However, in the dark recesses of the convolutions of my brain lurked a fervent wish that after passage of so much time they would have decided instead to take up permanent residence in Switzerland or the Shetland Islands. Or, perhaps, they would have visited Jack Finney's Acme Travel Bureau on W. 42nd Street in Manhattan, in "Of Missing Persons," stated their desire to "escape," and received a folder and story about another planet, "Enchanting Verna, where life is the way it *should* be." Thereafter, they would have been whisked away by an energy ray to happily live the rest of their lives in true peace and harmony ... and not, as Damon Knight suggested in "To Serve Man," as livestock being cultivated to feed their alien planet's people.

In either case, I would have expected them to have thoughtfully, graciously signed the house lock, stock, and rain barrel over to me prior to their departure. And I would have expressed my heart-felt appreciation. "Oh, how very kind of you. So incredibly thoughtful of you. Thank you, thank you, thank you. Kiss-kiss. (I hoped you've already paid the mortgage in full.) Kiss-kiss."

It's not that I was entranced by the house. I wasn't. Not to cast aspersions, it was what you'd expect of a cookie-cutter house built in the early 1960s as the suburbs expanded post-World War Two. With silver-green vertical siding, it boasted its floor levels being staggered. You know, two short sets of stairs on the left, one running up toward to the additional bedrooms and one leading down to the finished basement, which had been converted into a small game room and laundry area and was next to the attached one-car garage. The front door which opened into the living room, kitchen, and master bedroom was on the second level. The house was larger than I needed but provided the basics for shelter and life. I wanted it because ... well, I didn't want to move. I mean, I *really* didn't want to move.

Moving brought back memories of when I was four years old, before everything went awry. I was born in Summit, New Jersey, and we had already rented houses in Florham Park and Madison. My father had secured a building loan from his wealthy father, who was a sales executive with the Parker Pen Company, headquartered in Manhattan, to build our very first house in Summit. We were so excited. When the construction was finished, my bedroom closet had my long-desired, small hexagonal window. This represented my portal to nirvana even before I knew what a transcendent state felt like or was supposed to be. I suspect early childhood is the most likely time when this non-karmic moment of no suffering, no desire, no sense of self exists. Then things changed.

Near the end of our first year, my grandfather dropped a grenade with the firing pin removed at our feet. At first, he had been hinting, then he started bellyaching, that in order for him to buy yet another Cadillac, the newest model status symbol to add to his stable of his sleek, black cars, he'd *have* to dip into his bank account which he *just* didn't want to do. Wink, wink. Nudge, nudge. He claimed, "Actually, it would be a much smarter financial move for me to call in what's owed me. So, I want you to immediately repay the construction loan in its totality."

Since they had verbally-contracted a seven-year loan, my father was stunned, speechless. He had finally demonstrated to us that he could support us as he felt he was expected to do. He explained what my grandfather already knew, that since we needed the loan, we didn't have the money to repay him right then, but we could do it somewhat earlier than what their agreement had called for. I don't know if it ever consciously occurred to my father that his self-indulgent father was, in truth, asking him to volunteer to sacrifice our new home—a *house*, for crying out loud—for dear ol' granddad's new toy. When my father didn't volunteer right away, my grandfather proposed, "If you don't have the cash, I can wait—but not very long—just until you *sell* the house."

In retrospect, I have wondered if my grandfather would have sued his own son for the money if my father had balked. But my father would never have balked. Like his two brothers, he was intimidated, in fact, truly afraid of his father. I don't know if each had spit on his hand and then shaken on their verbal agreement, but I knew we considered it legally binding. My grandfather was one who believed in power and entitlement, that the rules that applied to the rest of us mere mortals did not apply to him.

Gone in a flash was my hexagonal closet window. Gone was my mother's brilliantly-executed, floriferous rock garden in the backyard that rains had destroyed twice only to be re-built even better. Gone was my father's professionally-mowed, Pebble Beach Golf Links-like grass of which he was so proud. Gone was *our* first, and last, house ... ever.

After that, I slowly became interested in architecture, thinking that perhaps that one day I could build my own house. It would be all mine. It would not be at risk in anyway of being seized. It would not be beholden to anyone.

In my adolescence my architectural yearnings leaned toward buildings from the Bauhaus School to Frank Lloyd Wright, especially Wright's 1935 cantilevered masterpiece, "Fallingwater." While gorgeous, the house was way beyond my perceived future ability to execute, much less pay for. I had to scale down.

Later I designed a concrete-formed round house, reminiscent of architect Charles Deaton's 1966 concrete Sculptured House, an elliptical curved house which is also referred to as the "Spaceship House." It was used in Woody Allen's 1973 film, "Sleeper." Located on Genesee Mountain, west of Denver, it looks like a taco or smiling clam with a dramatic wrap-around, glass-enclosed deck. I lusted after that controversial construction, thinking maybe that was a possibility on a much smaller scale. I really didn't need five levels, covering 7,700 square feet, with five bedrooms and five bathrooms.

In my early twenties I became inspired by architect Philip Johnson's glass house which he built in New Canaan, Connecticut, in 1949. This iconic minimalist house, which is now a tourist attraction, is a modern simple cube, consisting of 1,815 square feet of floor space, totally surrounded by glass. It is integrated into its forty-nine-acre, serene, park-like promontory landscape. In spite of its historic modernity, it has a traditional single-floor layout, except, of course, for the absence of walls. There is, however, a solid core floating bathroom in the middle of the house. All the utilities are congregated in a somewhat hidden, low brick building off at a short distance from the house. With having glass walls, apparently privacy wasn't an important consideration for Johnson who lived there from 1949 until his death at ninety-eight in 2005.

For me, being constantly exposed to the outside world, irrespective of its setting within many acres of wooded and tranquil surroundings, was a big drawback. And while I wouldn't think of spoiling its unique look with draperies or Venetian blinds, at the same time, I wouldn't relish wearing an ankle-length trench coat all the time either. I mean, there would be times when I'd want shed it to shake my naked booty as I tarantella-ed around the floor, especially when a tempestuous squall was percolating outside. There are times when it is deliciously hedonistic to dance *in* the rain … and times when being soggy and covered in goose bumps takes the sensuous edge off it fast.

The bed being visible from three sides also gave me pause so I reconsidered. After all, when I won the lottery and became one of the financial "one percent," I didn't need to spend my "millions" to reproduce his home as my own. Besides, over time my previous desire for oodles and oodles of open space quietly transmuted into less is more, perhaps reflective of a sort of cocooning where simplicity and "owning less stuff" became appealing. Now I'm at a point in my life where I sometimes think that a six-hundred-square-foot wood yurt could potentially suffice, as long as it had good storage space—you can't get rid of everything.

Despite the inconveniences and lack of architectural pizzazz of the Willow Road house, it had become *home*. My feet had taken root. The neighborhood was tree-enshrouded and devoid of fast cars and the guttural vroom of engine-revving motorcycles (whether Harley-Davidsons or Indians or …) which thunderously had roared up and down the streets of Millis, Massachusetts, when I was a teenager. They were not only putting domestic and wild animals at risk but also quickly destroying any sense of peace and placidity, not that my angst-filled teenage years were remotely placid otherwise.

My yard—yes, that's how I had come to think of it—was graced with a verdant lushness of azaleas, rhododendrons, and maple and oak trees around the perimeter in back and on the sides. Two mature maples stood in the front yard adding style and grace. The grass which surrounded the house always produced the most seductive hay-like scent when cut with a hand mower. That reminded me of the time after *our* house was finished in the summer. I would lie across my small bed with the window open as my father mowed the regulated front yard. He mowed high and often, taking off about one-third of the length of the grass, resulting in an attractive, neatly trimmed lawn, and the yummiest smell of plant-released volatile organic compounds we call "newly-mown grass."

2

MEMORIES OF HOME

Faust savored everything about the Sudbury yard too. Whenever he could, he spent his outdoor time eyeballing and leaping after grasshoppers or half-heartedly chasing his antagonist, a vision-impaired squirrel I had named "Rooster" after eye-patch-wearing John Wayne as "Rooster Cogburn" in 1969 *True Grit*. He also enjoyed locating other animal scents. Often, he curled back his upper lip, exposing his fangs, inhaled with his nostrils closed, and remained unmoving for several seconds as chemical messages drifted across his vomeronasal organ, part of his olfactory sensory system. This flehmen response, found in most mammals, though questionable in humans, was an attempt to detect passing pheromones from individuals of the same species which suggested reproduction or social behavior.

But his favorite activity, aside from performing his many "tricks," was libidinously rolling in the grass, cut or uncut. Even in his leash and harness, he would flop over onto his back and orgasmicly wiggle his spine from shoulders to tail, over and over again. He reminded me of a tomato hornworm on a Beefsteak branch gyrating to stretch itself to reach a next new leaf to devour it on its ravenous journey toward achieving hummingbird-moth-hood status.

Faust has been my feline house mate and companion since 1976. Strangely enough, our relationship began with a figurative kidnapping. Well, not in your every-day parlance or law book definition of the word. Yet it did evolve through one's using cunning and manipulation to make me a captive.

One evening as I left Sudbury's Goodnow Library after giving a presentation, I was unexpectedly confronted in the parking lot. Wearing a ratty gray coat that hugged his skeletal body, this creature squeezed out from under my avocado green VW Rabbit. Wheezing, he rubbed against my ankles to get my attention. Startled, I focused on his gaunt scabby skull, ear-mite-blackened inner ears, and distinct vampire teeth. They held me fast as I questioned myself about what I should do. From his look and sound, he was clearly going to be shuffling off this mortal coil in the not too distant future. Still, his amber eyes held a glint—a mesmerizing sparkle—that contradicted my assumptions. It suggested that no matter how smart I thought I was in my analysis, he wasn't quite ready to relinquish what was left of his life.

In only a few seconds of our encounter, I knew I had been afflicted by the Stockholm Syndrome. I felt empathy, sympathy, and positive feelings about my captor. Defending and identifying with him, I couldn't escape. No, it was in fact that I *chose* not to escape from him. For whatever time was left for him, we were meant to be together ... as soul mates. And as melodramatic as it sounds, I had, in effect, become my captor's slave. Well, actually, more like his servant. Thus began the sometimes-wild saga of my life with the soon-to-be Faust the Dancing Cat.

In my yard it would be hard for Faust to leave the eight-foot tall flowering dogwood that he had loved to climb over the years, no matter the season. Its scarred bark bore witness to his frequent scaling endeavors. In the warmer months he took to practicing his Flying Wallendas' high-wire act along its branches. Fearless, like the Wallendas, he also worked without a net. Though, I'm sure he correctly thought of me as also serving that function. After all, what are domestic help for. As time went on, he became a somewhat successful daredevil-stunt performer.

The only dangerous Wallendas' stunt he was never going to try was the high-wire pyramid. The sticking point was not the risk or danger. No, Faust was inured to such possibilities. It was that it would have required the participation of another critter or two. That would not have worked. Faust was an individualist, a non-conformist. When on stage, he was a soloist, "a cat alone."

As he rehearsed in the dogwood, one of my many tasks was to carefully manage to keep his leash from tangling in branches and twigs, and potentially hanging him, or interfering with his deliberate foot placement. While I'm sure Faust would wholeheartedly disagree, it seemed to me he never quite progressed beyond having less than three paws on his limb of choice for *more* than a nanosecond. However, during that billionth of a second, he reared like the Lone Ranger's horse, Silver. That was awesome to behold.

This was particularly impressive since he was balancing on a nubby, irregular cylindrical surface, unlike the living room floor where he labored over most of his Gene Kelly gymnastics. Maybe if he'd been motivated to practice more religiously, he could have executed his bipedal stand for a second or two. If he could have then traversed the branch in a vertical position, that would have been his golden ticket to tinsel town via a spot on the Ed Sullivan Show, if only it hadn't ended in 1971. There was always the carnival circuit but he would, no doubt, have considered that crass and beneath him. After all, Faust was an "artiste." But he did whatever he did because he enjoyed it. It wasn't work to him. But once practice slipped over into the realm of labor, a struggle, or chore, forget it. Fortunately, that apparently never happened. He could thank me for that, if I say so myself.

This high-wire skill acquisition was in addition to his many other stellar feats, like performing the Viennese waltz. Even without out a tuxedo, diamond shirt studs, bow tie, and red cummerbund, his was a classic presentation. Over time he had mastered the dance's three-beat time. Never moving his hips and almost flexing his kitty knees, he seemed to swing through the movement. The only aspect of his execution that he never managed to master was direction. *Oh-so-shockingly*, he always danced clockwise instead of the required counter-clockwise— the ultimate no-no at the Harvest Moon Ball Dance Championships—much to his chagrin.

Faust had established his roots in the house as well. He had spent his years with me painstakingly exploring every nook and cranny for the hint of a cockroach or a beady-eyed mouse. He seemed to have the structure totally mapped out, both visually and auditorily. As a result, when an unusual sound occurred, his antennae drew him immediately to the precise location to surprise the culprit, which, sometimes, he didn't expect.

When Rooster, who resided in the forty-foot maple towering along the backyard property line, tapped on the living room's back window, Faust magically appeared at the location. Hopping on to the windowsill, he glared at the sassy intruder with his right eye open and the left closed. This, I assumed, was the feline version of the hairy eyeball. Rooster stared back at him arrogantly. As if to further taunt Faust, he tapped the window again with his front claws and chattered what seemed to me like "nyaggh, nyaggh, nyaggh" in squirrel-ese.

An incensed Faust paced the windowsill in response. He looked to be ruminating upon Rooster's demise, perhaps as a bowl of squirrel stew, either bourguignon or goulash. When he stopped, pacing he seemed undecided about what to do next. As Rooster continued to tap the pane higher then lower, Faust pulled his lips back and made a chuffing sound. Rooster scrutinized this pathetic maneuver and, I swear, shook his head dismissively. With his fluffed-out tail waving in Faust's face, he scampered away. Poor Faust. So near yet so far. The indignity of it all.

After we had received the renting death knell, Faust and I had searched and searched real estate. As usual, Faust accompanied me on each jaunt, wrapped around my shoulders wherever I went. This clearly did not please some realtors who made their disdain known by snide remarks or curling their upper lip as if smelling camembert cheese, an odor often described as a cross between flatulence and fetid feet. Making the search even more difficult was my preference for renting a house rather than an apartment. But house rental pickings were poor.

As a social psychologist and coach with counseling training, I currently saw clients in the Willow Road game room which I dedicated for that purpose because it was quiet and private. Three comfortable stuffed chairs set around a fruitwood coffee table at the center with a water carafe and glasses, plants on stands, and soothing original oil paintings on the walls. Ambiance can make a difference in level of attentiveness and willingness to progress.

Faust's presence, in some instances, made it easier for clients to listen, express themselves, ask questions, and share. Also, sometimes petting and playing with him relaxed and comforted them when dealing with difficult issues. Other times he provided them a reward for having a good session. Occasionally, however, his presence interfered with their concentration or desire to work on their skills and issues. It was a difficult balancing act, when to have him present and when not to. It was trial and error with each client.

One time when I wanted to remove Faust from a particularly sensitive session, he mohwed (his version of "meow") and slapped his carrier, demonstrating he thought he should be present all the time. Ironically, his indignant behavior was the right note to get the session back on track. The client laughed and hugged the disbelieving cat.

Beneficially, the returning owners had kindly given us a month and a half lead time to "make all my rental dreams come true." It helped because it took additional weeks to finally locate the current house in Wellesley. The house I settled on there was oddly configured and not ideal by any stretch of the imagination. The big plus for Faust was its two-level lawn, lots of trees, including a gnarled apple tree, and abundant wildlife.

When we first saw it, Faust responded as if he would have laid down his life to get it. As we approached it, his claws expressed his ecstatic anticipation of exploration and discovery as he intensely surveyed it from his perch on my right shoulder. The scars from his decision remain to this day. While deficient in a number of ways, from a practical standpoint the house did have a good location, a heavily-treed suburban community, not far from Boston. I reconciled myself that being closer to the city it was closer to an expanded pool of potential clients.

Still, moving meant that I'd have to essentially re-establish myself to reach all these new people. This would be time-consuming and b-o-r-i-n-g. My interpersonal communications coaching and social marketing consulting business was *finally* seeing the light of black ink so being unceremoniously uprooted and replanted would entail all sorts of vexations. I wasn't looking forward to contacting all my individual and business clients to apprise them of their upcoming driving inconvenience. Since most of them lived in or worked around Sudbury or west of there, they would be facing another twenty-five miles to meet with me. I had to ask myself: Even if they thought of me as the world's best strawberry shortcake, made with giant, luscious strawberries from Watsonville, California, and slathered with gobs and gobs of fresh whipped cream, would they really want to have to drive that additional distance to continue to have it? Would I? As much as I liked me, *I'd* have to give that some hard thought.

3

THE MOVE

Once I grudgingly agreed with Faust on the house, it had taken some negotiation with the owners to produce a mutually-agreeable leasing contract. First, they had to alleviate some of the most concerning problems, like its lacking appreciable insulation. This 1924, two-story house was going to be a money pit, heating-wise, without loads of the Pink Panther's Fiberglas battens to help. Since the house had been on the market for a lengthy period of time and was quickly becoming a realtor's white elephant, there was, hopefully, some room for compromise.

Adding insulation to floors, ceilings, basement, and attic was more an obstacle than the eviction of the flourishing mice population in the basement. I didn't tell Faust about the upcoming mouse expulsion because when we initially checked out the house, he had been thrilled with the critters skittering around the kitchen floor after oozing under the door from the basement. It was more an omission than a lie, I kept guiltily telling myself.

In addition, capping the chimney was a necessity to prevent the raccoons, which daily paraded across the roof, from an overhanging maple bough in the backyard, from scaling the chimney, slithering down it into the living room fireplace, and leaving ghost-like ash footprints on the hardwood floors. As much as I loved animals, I had no desire to become a raccoon wrangler. And Faust would certainly have wanted to give it a try, much to his resulting displeasure, I was sure. It was a safe bet that the raccoons, after having slid twenty-some feet down an early-Twentieth Century-era flue and thumped hard onto a brick hearth, with or without andirons, would not have been thrilled with any foolhardy soul attempting to corral them to escort them outside.

Even though they had wanted me to sign up for at least three years in exchange for their financial outlay, I contracted for a two-year lease, renewable for one year at a time thereafter. I didn't want to feel stifled, stuck, or controlled. As much as I hated moving, it was theoretically possible that I might find a better location later ... *much* later.

And contrary to reality, even after my having experienced California's earthquakes, wildfires, and death-defying fogbanks first-hand at an earlier time, the sparkling, magical images of the mythical California dream still swirled in my head and lingered in my daydreams, calling me back, in spite of its smog and bumper-to-bumper traffic day and night.

With the house search settled, before me in the here and

now was the joyous task of moving. Ptui! I'm sure some people don't mind moving, find it exciting, or somehow tolerate it. Faust was one. I wasn't. As a kid, I was always moving. At first when I was very young it was because of my father's sales job with the Parker Pen Company which moved him (and us) around territories in New Jersey then to ones in Pennsylvania. His father *required* that his three sons work for his company. It was both revolting and sad that his sons didn't dare say no to him and would do almost anything he "asked" in order to curry his favor, or avoid pain.

As a result, by the time I reached high school, I had attended thirteen schools, always the awkward newbie and outsider. And then before I knew it, I was on the road again. It was tough making friends and fitting in, especially in rural areas. Later our constant moving was because of my father's undiagnosed bi-polar disorder that kept us one step ahead of the law. One minute we were flush, the next penniless, so we continually skipped out on rent-due houses and apartments. I was mortified, hoping no one I knew would ever find out. Being a criminal wouldn't add to my already-suspect alien persona.

Even though it was irrelevant and inconsequential after all these years, my anticipated move brought it all back with a nauseating knot in my gut. I hadn't consciously recognized how traumatic it would feel being reminded of the humiliation and psychological trauma. So much of what moving represented to me was loss. Loss of hard-won, short-lived relationships. Loss of security. Loss of continuity and a sense of place.

Projecting my emotional distress onto Faust, I assumed he would be stressed out and fearful. On the contrary, Faust appeared delighted, totally in his element. He seemed to find it all part of an exciting new adventure. I thought the least he could do was empathize with me. But, no, he made the most of it. Consequently, while I was stressed out and exhausted from locating boxes, newsprint for wrapping, and shipping tape, then compartmentalizing what would go where, and finally packing so my possessions were safe and unlikely to shift, Faust was bounding about while pretending to supervise my efforts.

Cavorting from one box to another, he padded the paper protecting its contents into corners. He tore out pieces, large and small that he seemed to think didn't fit his kitty paradigm of perfection. Some he chewed on. That stymied me. Was he attempting to make wood filler, using the wood fibers in the paper and binding them with spit? If so, for what purpose? Attempting to understand humans was hard enough but "understanding" the machinations of a cat, even one as human-like as Faust, seemed, sometimes, nearly impossible. Then he tossed some of the torn pieces into the air and hit them as they descended. Those that went sideways he ignored. But those that came down to him, he punched again upward, in a verisimilitude of beach volleyball.

In general, I wondered if all his packing box behaviors were his way of letting me know he thought I was not doing the job properly. That was a possibility: That he was indicating that … and that it was true. However, in my near-fugue state, I neither needed nor appreciated his chastising me. My cat the critic. Puh-leeze. By the time I was done with packing, I had regressed to childhood petulance and was wallowing in self-pity. I was acting as if I had a special license to *suffer*. And, so I did, brow furrowed and lower lip protruding.

For the move, I had rented the fifteen-foot U-Haul to accommodate all my own furniture, some of which I used in the furnished rental. But my other furniture, dozens of previously-packed boxes of books, dishes, pots and pans, and miscellany I had were stored, floor to ceiling, in the second bedroom on the third level. The tiny one-car garage, replete with insects and rodents, had been spared. At least I didn't have to pack the contents of all those existing boxes. Something for which I was grateful.

To pick up the truck a neighbor had driven me over to the gas station where the trucks were stored. When I arrived home, Faust was standing on the back of the stuffed chair by the front picture window, wiggling his butt with glee, his tail switching back and forth. Almost any novelty grabbed and held his attention until he could check it out. Curiosity today held him tightly in its grip. Being an understanding kitty mom, I let him explore the back of the truck which consisted of the one hundred and seventeen square feet of new and exotic smells.

He tried to scratch his way up the interior's intermittently-corrugated metal sides to grab hold of the tie-downs. But he kept slipping down, his claws making fist-clenching, sinus-grating sounds. As his frustration increased, I finally helped him scramble into Mom's Attic, the fifty-four cubic feet of jammed additional space, which hung over the cab.

Initially I had thought I'd need a car trailer if I couldn't find some assistance for doing the actual move. But having secured the assistance of two neighborhood men, I no longer needed to. Fortunately, two fathers who lived near me volunteered to pack the truck and unload on the other end. One, Gordon Swarthout, a fifty-something electrical engineer, had looked upon me as a daughter clone. His own daughter, Colleen, had moved away to Hartford, Connecticut, gone to Yale, gotten a job at a Wall Street law firm, gotten married to another attorney, Jim, had two children, Bernice and Arthur, and was now too busy juggling all the aspects of her life to visit him with any frequency. The other was Michael Finster, his next-door neighbor who worked in IT in Cambridge. It was his creative seven-year-old girl, Jennie, I'd introduced to writing memoirs about her dog, Little Bit, two cats, Ollie and Harry, and a parakeet, Nipper.

At 10 a.m., Faust and I left Sudbury for Wellesley … forever … in my fully-packed Rabbit. Ostensibly Faust was acting guard over my luggage and boxes of clothing, linens, and dishes in the car's rear compartment where I had folded the back seats down flat. He sniffed, pawed, and raked the cardboard, renting it, and strewing the pieces everywhere. I could hear the clear 3M shipping tape being stretched, screeching like a tortured living creature trying not to yield to his talons.

He was acting as if he were convinced that there were Faust-designated goodies hidden therein, that the sealed boxes represented the avenues of his treasure hunt. At this moment I regretted having introduced him to hide-and-seek with kitty prizes. As I drove, he feverishly scratched and tore at the cardboard boxes. If I'd been more attuned to him instead of to myself as I contemplated how I'd handle the unloading, where I'd have everything stored or placed, I would have recognized that wasn't what he was doing. Maybe he suddenly recognized he was leaving what had always been his home since I had rescued him … and felt bereft and, maybe, a little anxious. I knew that feeling.

But … Hold on a second. He was a *cat*. Sure, he was allowed to be anxious and depressed. But the more he destroyed the cardboard boxes, the more I had to acknowledge that he might simply have been showing his displeasure. Not necessarily at leaving "the old homestead," but maybe at not having access to the empty car wherein he could roam at will when the spirit moved him. Maybe he was feeling squashed with no space to spread out and get comfortable. Maybe he was unhappy at not being able to ride in the back of the truck where he could further explore. I was, perhaps, interfering with his basic feline desires and creature comforts. He had repeatedly shown that as long as he could do what he wanted, he didn't seem to give a rat's butt *why* we did what we did.

Gordon, who lived two houses down Willow Road, drove the truck while Mike drove in his car behind the truck to help unload. At the Wellesley house they hauled all pieces of furniture up the long, concrete-slab walkway and up the sharp left-hand stairs to the front door, then into to their respective rooms.

Once inside, getting the box spring and mattress up the narrow and dog-leg-to-the-right staircase was a sweat fest. This was, especially since Faust wouldn't stop doing figure eights around their legs as he tried to snag the mattress's tag. It wasn't until Gordon cried out, "Help!" that I knew Faust had extricated himself from the half-bath off the kitchen, where I'd held him captive. He's simply pushed on the bi-fold door to open it. I rushed to the constricted staircase area and squeezed under the mattress, praying they wouldn't lose their grip as I tried to disconnect Faust who was being dragged, thumping up the stairs, by his claws.

I had them dump all the boxes unceremoniously in the dining room. This was through the sun room, the space which would have been a foyer in a more upmarket house, around the corner of the living room, and on their immediate right. When we finished, including the stuff in my car, I fixed them lunch—well, if you can call Campbells' tomato soup, plain saltines, with tap water to drink "lunch." After their "gourmet" repast, they headed out to drop off the truck and then return home in Michael's car.

With the dining room as unloading central, I was able to comfortably navigate around the rest of the house. Despite the opened and unopened boxes, stacked at the rear of the dining room, under the windows facing onto the backyard, I had managed to set the room's few essentials in place. The circular maple table and two captain's chairs were against the center of the dining room-kitchen wall. The Panasonic 17-inch CRT television was set up on the Building 19 TV cart I had purchased with my Technics turntable underneath on the front outside wall. The KLH speakers for the turntable were currently languishing on the floor on either side of the TV cart until I could figure out where to put them. A stuffed chair in several earth tones was located across from the television for Faust and my viewing. There was also a teak bookshelf, the twin of one I put in the living room, against the outside entry wall.

Because there was a painted-white swinging door between the dining room and kitchen, I had had Gordon and Michael slip it off its hinges, and place it in the basement, to protect Faust. His habit of following close behind me would put him in danger of being squished as the opened door swung back.

After Gordon and Mike departed, Faust was once again attacking the crumpled newsprint that boiled out of the boxes, vaulting in and out of empty and partially-unloaded boxes, pretending to hide from the neighboring wildlife, and attacking lurking invisible predators, as well as my ankles when I walked by. His frolicking was making the situation lighter and more positive. But I wasn't in the mood for "lighter and more positive."

It wasn't so much that I begrudged Faust his play time. Well, yeah, actually I did. I was tired, sweaty, grubby, and depressed. It seemed to me that he could have used his hyperactive paws to unwrap the dishes, pots, and pans. And then if he felt so inclined, he could then have dragged them into the kitchen. It's not that I expected him to climb on to the counters with them to put them away, but he was overdoing his slothful dancing grasshopper routine to my dour, over-achieving ant's.

Since the kitchen lacked any food preparation work space to the right of the gas range, I had already arranged for delivery of a four-foot-long cabinet I knew I'd need the moment I had first laid eyes on this long, misshapen kitchen. The existing countertops that were nearly six feet across the room from the stove wouldn't do. To the left of the stove I placed a thirty-six-inch tall, one-drawer cabinet to have a spot on which to put items I'd taken from the refrigerator to my left. The refrigerator backed onto the tiny wall segment, between the door to the living room and the swinging door to the dining room. This was not your convenient or utilitarian kitchen. I guarantee Julia Child would not have approved.

4

ADJUSTING

Despite all my measured, architectural-style drawings that I had made of the front room, before renting the Wellesley house, that spoke to the inadvisability of using that space as my office, I still tried to arrange the twelve-by-ten room as a place I could meet with clients and handle business. But even using small-size furniture (two very small chairs with an end table in between, a small rectangular table for my desk and computer on the far wall, and a bookcase between two closet doors), it was going to be snug.

Facing the street were three windows with a radiator underneath, making that three-foot space unusable for anything else. While I like small, efficient places, this room would have taken a miracle to resemble an operational office. But as Einstein said, "The measure of intelligence is the ability to change." I'd figure out something, somehow. I was sure he included "adapting" and "accommodating" in his definition.

Faust oversaw my attempts to make the previous sun room

into business space. After careful deliberation, he selected the client's mini-chair next to radiator as his own. That required my putting a red washable cover on it to be able to easily and quickly remove his cat hair for clients. Whether or not my clients loved cats, I knew they wouldn't love to have their clothing covered in clingy gray fur every time they came for a session.

The radiator was well-kept—no peeling white paint or gouges—but it was ugly. It needed to be covered. After purchasing an off-white steel radiator cover for it, I placed various houseplants on it. Faust particularly liked the green-and-white-striped spider plant. He spent endless hours exercising his right front paw batting the leaves of new young plants which hung on long, arcing stems. When he tired of emulating Hank Aaron or Muhammad Ali, he chewed on the leaves then regurgitated them on the radiator cover or bare wood floor beneath. When the radiator was on and warm, cleaning up the stomach-juice-Osterized plant-material, aka kitty puke, *immediately* was essential. Otherwise, it would dry permanently glued to the thin metal, adding a unique but distasteful design and texture to it.

I loved having plants around me. But picking indoor plants for the office and the rest of the house was more difficult than I expected. I wanted plants that were attractive, easy to care for, and, above all, safe for cats. At the Wellesley Free Library on Washington Street I discovered what the ASPCA, the American Society for the Prevention of Cruelty to Animals, had to say. According to their experts, the spider plant was considered non-toxic, or, perhaps, better described as non-lethal, to cats and other pets.

However, eating the leaves might pose a potential risk. This is because spider plants contain chemical compounds related to opium which can cause stomach upset, vomiting, and diarrhea. In general, the recommendation is to keep cats away from the plant. Of course, like people, all cats are different and what affects one mildly may affect another more severely. Fortunately, Faust had only mild digestive irritation which, apparently, was not objectionable enough to him to prevent his desiring to have yet another chomp. This he happily did over and over, regurgitating as a result, and rendering the poor plant mauled and ragged-looking.

In spite of the fact that there are a lot of plants that are toxic to cats, there are a good number that aren't. Non-toxic houseplants included African violet, bamboo, Boston fern, bromeliads, burros tail sedum, cast iron plant (Aspidistra), Christmas cactus, Haworthia succulents which are similar to aloe, palms (areca, bamboo, parlor, pony tail), peperomia, phalaenopsis orchid, prayer plant (Marantha), and Swedish ivy. That would give me lots of options. I'd try one than another to see how Faust responded, keeping my fingers crossed. I put the ASPCA Animal Poison Control phone number, 888-426-4435, on my refrigerator and upstairs phone for quick reference, which, as it turned out, I would need.

Before we went to bed one evening shortly after we had moved in, I took Faust into the yard for a romp. He scampered up the apple tree which would soon become a playhouse for him, rolled on the grass, chased imaginary prey, and nibbled on some flowers. I'd locked up, turned off the lights, and was just getting into bed to join him. He sat on the bed looking at me oddly … then collapsed. His body went stiff. He went into convulsions. Uncontrolled muscle contractions made him jerk. His paws paddled. His jaws snapped.

While cat seizures are said to typically last only a minute or two, his were continuing. I called the ASPCA poison line then took the stairs down two at a time to get the phone book. I had to find an animal emergency clinic. Back upstairs, grabbed his seizing body. His bladder let loose, soaking the man's t-shirt I wore to bed. I lay him back down on the bed, threw off the t-shirt, slid on a sweatshirt and jeans, and slipped into my Bass Weejuns. Back in the kitchen I stuffed him into his carrier. I ran to the basement to the garage. As I was getting the garage door raised, I saw a bag of Sevin Pesticide. It was for fruits, vegetables, and flowers. The flowers he ate? Had they been sprayed with this? Oh, crap! That stuff was lethal. It could last on plants for months.

It took me twenty minutes, well exceeding the speed limit on local roads, to find the ER near the Natick line. The moment I was inside, I shouted, "He's been poisoned. By Sevin Pesticide, I think."

Instantly his carrier disappeared. I was unable to read a magazine or sit still. I ran his activities through my mind. Could it have been anything else? Nothing came to mind. I wanted to pace but received frowns and comments to sit down as I made a second round of the room. As I sat, I kept jiggling my right leg. The woman next to me, said brusquely, "Would you please stop that?" I repeatedly asked myself, "Am I going to lose him?" After a half-hour of sweating and trying not to cry, I saw someone who looked like a veterinarian.

She looked over the assembled and asked, "Is Faust's guardian here?" I raised my hand and she called me over. "You can relax now. He's going to be okay. I gave him an injection of atropine. That particular insecticide inhibits specific enzymes from breaking down a neurotransmitter, acetylcholine. When it can't be broken down normally, the result is unending nervous transmission to the muscles, among other things, which causes the seizures. Atropine is an antagonist which reverses the unending transmission. It's a good thing you got him here so quickly and had an idea what the poison might have been."

"I just literally stumbled across the bag in the garage of the house I rent before getting here. Yes, that was my incredible luck."

"I suggest you find a container you can close tightly to put the bag in. Wearing gloves and a mask would be the safe way to do it since it's a fine powder. Hosing down those areas you think might have been sprayed may help a little, although, unfortunately, that will still leave residue on the grass and ground. Perhaps the owner can tell you more specifically what items were sprayed and when."

I practically dislocated her shoulder shaking her hand, thanking her for saving Faust. That was too close for comfort. I'd never felt so helpless before with respect to him. It was midnight when I finally opened the car door again. I put Faust 's carrier on the passenger seat, slid into the driver's seat, keeping a hand on his carrier to protect it, and we headed home … and finally to bed. But not to sleep. I was afraid not to watch him closely until morning just in case the atropine didn't do the whole job or something else happened. However, it didn't. He was fine the next morning. Yawning and looking like I'd slept on my face, I wished I had been fine too. I wondered what else that was potentially dangerous might have been used in or around the house recently that I didn't know about. I just hoped all the exterminated mice in the basement had been collected. I didn't want him poisoned again by munching on one. I'd have to give it a cursory look. I'd really look forward to that.

5

BREAKING INTO CABLE

Continental Cablevision had recently arrived in Wellesley and announced that it was looking for original proposals for community programs. After checking to see what programs they already had, I proposed "The Inside Track," a thirty-minute alternative-career development interview program which would present interesting business and trade people and professionals to talk about what they did, how they learned about it, what they needed to do to prepare for it, and how they actually got into it. They provided advice for how others could follow their lead, emphasizing inside information. If they had a product or service they wanted to share, they would give a short promo too. My show had two purposes. One was to educate people in the community who wanted to enter a career or change jobs or careers. The other was to give Faust visibility and myself credibility.

As producer and host, I had to find and choose these guests, prepare relevant questions for them based upon visiting with them and lots of research on them and their fields.

If they had a book, I had to read and fully understand it so I could ask useful, informative questions about their topics. It took a lot of time and effort. Faust often helped me by rectally reading these materials and sharing his assessment. My continuing lament was that he didn't speak English better.

However, before I could actually produce my own show, I had to be trained in all aspects of cable television production and what a show, any show, required to make it work. I had to learn about lighting equipment and then how to appropriately light the set, when to open and close barn-doors on lights and when to use filters. How to create the best set for viewing for each show. Where to place microphones on guests and how to test voice levels of both guests and the host. Where to place coaxial cables and duct-tape them to the floor for both safety and so they wouldn't interfere with camera movement.

Then, of course, I had to learn how to use video cameras, white balance them, when to pan or zoom, how to roll the wheeled camera tripods. How to create graphics for the show itself and its guests and when to use them. Then I had to learn about the control room which could be at the studio or in the station's fully-equipped van for remote broadcast locations. That included its monitors of camera views, audio control, switching from one camera to another, and electro-graphics machine for creating on-screen names and labels. Finally, I had to produce a ten-minute video I had scripted. I did that at the Wellesley City Hall where I pretended to be part of the community questioning city officials on traffic improvement. It went well until at the very end when I thought the camera had completed the shoot and I looked directly into the camera lens with a silly smile. Duh! Note to me: Always stay in character. It's a good thing videotape was "malleable."

After all this, I had to crew other people's shows … first. As a crew member, one had to arrive about an hour ahead of time depending upon the show and its location. Programs outdoors, like sports activities, were tricky because of weather and difficulty of set up. As time went on, when I wasn't a camera operator on the stage or in the aisle for Wellesley Symphony Orchestra concerts held at the Massachusetts Bay Community College, I was in the van sometimes directing or acting as technical assistant. Thus, before I did my first "Inside Track," I had crewed for numbers of shows which pretty much required all the same tasks in the same sequence.

In preparation for my show, I used my business and social network to find guests and/or referrals for guests. My guests included lawyers, entrepreneurs, authors, service providers, surgeon, politician, psychologist, large and small business people, veterinarian, actors, engineers, musicians, et al. Every single person I asked to be my guest said "yes" so I began with a long list of potential upcoming guests.

Then I had to meet them well ahead of time to determine what they wanted to share within the show's context, how they wanted to do it, and then schedule them. For each guest I created a script with my questions, timing for me and my guest's answers, what camera angles to use, when breaks occurred, what personalized set graphics might be employed (displayed books, posters, slides, videos, or audios) as well as their timing. Included at the end was a two-minute commercial by the guest just before I wrapped up the show. The guest received a copy of the script about ten days prior to their appearance to allow them to request any additions or changes.

For my first show I had clinical psychologist, Dr. Jolene Ross, who was going to discuss cognitive-behavioral therapy — a favorite subject of mine since it was the basis of the techniques I employed. At the time she was working specifically with panic disorder and how one could best cope with it. She described how CBT worked as well as what benefits it could provide not only for panic disorder but also for other forms of anxiety. At that time, I was also working with her on her social marketing. The show was informative and went smoothly. We both were pleased.

In general, for each show my plan was to arrive thirty minutes early, before taping. As producer, I brought my own set decorations: a walnut-framed bamboo three-panel screen, a fake four-foot dieffenbachia floor plant in a large brass container, and a three-foot long by two-and-a-half-foot wide abstract painting I had done with a palette knife in shades of red, orange, yellow, green, and black. I set everything up on the raised stage with two chairs and a table next to the guest's chair for display of whatever the guest wanted to bring to show. When the guest was using slides, I brought a slide projector and screen, put in the slides, checked its operation, the light bulb, and the proper sequence of slides. Then I attached the remote and threaded it to the guest's chair for his or her operation.

Next, I would create the show's electro-graphics, typing in the guest's name, my name, the names of crew members, their positions, and contact information for me and Continental Cablevision at the end. I'd also provide the tech person who would display the electro-graphics on-screen at the appropriate times with my show's title image and the taped background music which I had supplied.

I would have my guests arrive by ten to the hour. After greeting them, I would retrieve water for them, show them the bathroom, and further explain how it would go, when the show was scheduled to be seen, and ask if they had any questions. The first show went fine despite our mutual anxieties. However, things metamorphosed into Dante's Sixth Circle of Hell the night of the second show taping.

Unaware of my heresy, I arrived thirty minutes before show and started putting my set together. At that moment the program manager shouted at me from across the large room. In front of all the crew members, she loudly and imperiously asked, "Just who do you think you are? This is the second time in a row you've come in late and *not* crewed your show!"

I was thunderstruck, totally stunned. Nothing in my cable television training, in written or verbal instructions, had said that in addition to all I had to do before each of my own shows, I had to come in an hour early … to sweat and get my on-camera clothes all grimy from unrolling and placing cable, relocating the moveable stage, setting up cameras, and climbing ladders to adjust lighting, searching for miscellaneous equipment and supplies, such as mic batteries.

"What?" I said. "No one had ever told me that I had to totally crew my own show as well. I already do the stage set up, all the electro-graphics, check on the music and program title graphic, and set up and check any audio-visual equipment, posters, book displays, and anything else the guest requires."

Following other snide responses which just slid past me in my comatose state, she concluded with a supercilious smirk was, "Well, you *should* have known."

"How," I asked, "could I have known if no one had told me?"

She just shook her head in a theatrical display of disgust at having to deal with slackers and half-wits, noisily turned on heel, and strode off.

My heart was galloping in my chest, my face was scarlet. I was sweating under my arms, between my breasts, and down my back My blouse under my sports jacket was now soggy, wrinkled, and sticking to me. I was so glad I hadn't brought Faust to the studio to my first shows to witness this. I wanted him there for other shows once the pattern was established. He could sit quietly on my lap or on a chair next to me. Or, if

37

necessary, curled at my feet.

For one show I had planned on having him sit on Don Wescott's lap. Don, who was an actor, sculptor, poet, writer, member of the American Federation of Television and Radio Artists, and a Screen Actors Guild board director, was best known as the voice-over legend, aka narrator, of PBS's *Nova*, and other programs and documentaries, such as *Antiques Roadshow, Masterpiece Theater, American Experience, Mystery, Evening at POPS*, and *Vietnam*. He also was a cat lover. As such, he had done an album of his cat poetry, some of which he was going to read with his wonderfully resonant voice. Delightful. Faust would have loved it. And he could have done a little dance for Don at the end of his reading. But now I was abashed and so glad Faust hadn't witnessed my being verbally attacked. I don't know what he would have done. He was my protector. Should I bring him to the studio as I'd planned? I wasn't so sure now.

As for my "mistake," I knew I wasn't perfect. I knew I made mistakes, especially with something new. While I didn't like "being imperfect," I did voluntarily admit to my errors, though without any gusto. But this was too much.

It reminded me that when we had just moved to Millis for my freshman year in high school, I was lonely. As an outsider in a small town, I had not as yet made any close friends. When I made the mistake of bemoaning this fact to my father, he stated it was my fault. According to him, "People don't like you. It's because you're critical and judgmental." These, he enlightened me, were my "deep-seated character flaws." Each time he took the opportunity to point this out to me he would justify his actions with a sanctimonious, "I'm telling you this for your own good." I felt crushed. Even though I knew better than to do so, I always looked to my father to approve of me.

It took me years of carefully monitoring and questioning myself to finally shake my belief in his profoundly-cutting assessment of me. Overtime I discovered that his accusations and pronouncements were more likely projections of his own negative characteristics and traits, his insecurity, his inability to stand up to his sadistic father to make his own life decisions, or his incapacity to support his own family. As I discovered later in my personal exploration, I had vicariously picked up some hints of his behaviors and attitudes which I then had to address. What a pain!

Still overwhelmed from the program manager's harangue, and feeling unjustly accused, I made the mistake of turning to a crew member I had often worked with on other shows and relied on her experience. Desperate for some sympathy, lamely I said, "How was I supposed to have known?"

She just looked at me hard and curtly replied, *"Everyone* knows that. We were here on time, waiting for you, doing *your* work for you." I was doubly shocked. I was playing to a cold house.

Even though I had worked with them all before, always on

time, grinding along with them, they'd apparently simply assumed I was now acting like a "diva," feeling entitled because I was a producer and host. I was beside myself, embarrassed, and still experiencing the lasting negative vibes of the nose-out-of-joint crew members all around me.

I suddenly had this overpowering, compulsive urge to further defend myself. No! Stop! I mentally grabbed myself by my jacket lapels. I knew that feebly continuing to beat my gums was futile. Besides, emphasizing that point about not having been told was dicey. It had been the program manager who had trained me and—big surprise—had *not* mentioned that requirement, even though she had known about my proposed program for some time before. Clenching my jaw, I inadvertently bit my tongue but kept my mouth shut.

I finished everything I had to do for the show, greeted my guest, Carleton Kendrick, licensed psychotherapist, who had a behavioral-nutritional program to stop smoking and "Stay-Quit." I tried hard to put what I considered the height of inappropriate management-employee communications behind me as soon as possible. I needed to calm down, appear relaxed on camera, and keep my mind on the topic at hand. I managed to get through the show without blundering materially. It was more luck than skill.

However, after the show, I took the program manager aside and asked respectfully, "In the future if there is anything—anything at all—I have done that you're unhappy about or think I should do differently, please tell me *privately*. I'm sure we can work it out."

What I wanted to do what shake the program manager until her teeth rattled. What she should have done was quietly take me aside the first time I arrived thirty minutes before my show and asked, "Were you delayed this evening? Puzzled, I would have said, "No." Then she could have asked, "Did you know you were expected to arrive an hour before to crew your own show? That's in addition to everything else you already do before the show." What she could also have told me was, "Those crewing your show are unhappy that you hadn't arrived early, as expected, to get all the other preparatory work done." That would have allowed me to know their unvoiced, negative feelings, perhaps apologize to them for my lack of awareness of the situation, and meet everyone's expectations from then on.

It seemed so reasonable to me that when a problem arises, the best approach is always to be civil, to show respect, get the employee's understanding of the situation, calmly convey to him or her what the problem is as the manager perceives it, and get the employee's commitment to correct the problem in the future. This means there is no knee-jerk acting on unfounded, invalid assumptions. No big public scene with screaming criticism, sarcasm, and public humiliation. No abusive flexing of the manager's power and status muscles. In other words, no muss, no fuss, and no hard feelings.

After that incident, I looked at the program manager differently. I had lost my sense of trust in her, feeling less respect for her and her level of "professionalism." I also tended to watch her reactions to myself, others, and issues even more. Over time it became obvious to me, as I focused more on her and less on myself as a newbie show producer/host, that she also was a neophyte in her position with all the insecurity and angst that entailed.

Consequently, I never again considered bringing Faust, even for Don Wescott's interview. That was a real shame because it would have been not only informative but also great entertainment. Faust might even have done several of his tricks at the end as we ran the credits over the guest and me talking. I was concerned that if the program manager verbally exploded, she might send him into a panic, to streak around the studio looking for escape. His visibility on cable wasn't worth the risk.

We continued to get along. However, any time I thought there might be a problem, I made a point of speaking quickly and quietly to her about it. Expressing the problem in terms of what *I* saw, how *I* felt about it, and what *I* wanted done— instead of using *you*-terms—helped reduce her potential feelings of being accused or attacked. But we never had another problem. Having to be on-guard all the time, while she was still there, took a lot of fun out of working on my show at Continental Cablevision. Still I continued to produce my show for four years.

Having complete control over who would be on and what they could do made things sometimes very interesting. One guest was local surgeon Dr. Paul F. Gryska with whom I talked about getting into medical school and becoming a physician. Off-hand, I shared that becoming a physician had always been my dream but that I had to drop out of pre-med at Baylor because my family's health and financial problems. To my amazement, he stated categorically, "If you had *really* wanted to go, you'd have found a way."

I was stunned, insulted, and embarrassed. I could only hope it wasn't obvious to my viewing audience. Maybe that worked for males, who were expected to be doctors, but was less likely to work for females, who were *not* expected to be doctors. Before I left Baylor, I had tried to get a loan through the university but was told, "If you became a doctor, you'd only leave medicine to get married and have children. That means you'd have taken away the medical school slot for a male who would have continued to work as a doctor." What a sexist crock! But what did I expect in the male-dominated 1960s?

In my case, I left Baylor University because my father was physically and emotionally ill, unemployed, and we were losing our house and car. Always domineering, he refused to let my mother work outside the home in spite of everything crashing down around them. To have a woman supporting him was just too distressing to his ego. Being the practical one, she finally ignored his decades if authoritarian commandments. She found two jobs and employed my used Ford convertible. This turquoise and white beauty with gleaming white upholstery had been a birthday present that I had gotten to use for only one week before leaving for college in Waco, Texas, driving up and down Main Street in Millis, with the top down, my long hair waving sensuously in the breeze.

Now it was her transportation. But her jobs weren't enough to sustain them. Since my brother who was four years my junior was in no position to do much, that left it to me. After I returned from one year at Baylor, I filled in the gap with several part-time jobs. That's what females were expected to do: Be nurturing and do whatever was necessary to help the family unit survive.

As part of Dr. Gryska's interview, we did a first on Continental Cablevision. We taped him performing a gastrointestinal operation at Newton-Wellesley Hospital to give viewers an idea of some of what some physicians did. Unfortunately, because we couldn't use an elevated platform in the operating room for the cameras to shoot down at the surgical field, most of the tape left a lot to be imagined despite his running narration. That was good fortune for the squeamish. They could watch it without taking Compazine, unless they let their expectations of blood and gore run wild. The closest to blood the viewers would get was the use of Betadine Scrub, a brownish antiseptic, antimicrobial cleanser made with povidone-iodine, on the surgical area. Big yawn.

The many others that I interviewed included Matthias Chaplin, who was Executive Housekeeping Operations Manager at Newton-Wellesley Hospital, who was the first black on Continental Cablevision, who discussed the multi-various tasks his position oversaw. State Senator Robert Marsh explained how to get into politics and public service. Jay Fialkov, entertainment lawyer for WGBH–PBS, detailed what his diverse field covered. Local dentist Lawrence DiBona and his daughter, who was training to be a dentist, discussed what was new in dentistry. Sociologist Alexandra Dundas Todd discussed her research and book on the cultural conflicts between doctors and their women patients and their health implications. And controversial marketer and business author, Dr. Jeffrey Lant talked about having multiple and diverse products and services which dovetailed with his consulting business.

6

PROTECTOR OF THE REALM

As the Wellesley house began taking shape, accommodating more or less to my needs, a former-friend from Framingham came to visit. I had known Danny from when I worked at Massachusetts Institute of Technology in the Mechanical Engineering Department. There I had worked on a thesaurus of textile terms for a project for the U.S. Department of Standards. Slim, 5'7" with wavy sandy hair, an upturned nose, and dimpled smile, he had been a computer programming student then. We had dated for a while. When I moved to San Diego, it was understood that he was going to be attending Stanford University in Palo Alto, near what would become Silicon Valley. So he'd be in California too, close enough to continue dating. Au contraire.

After I departed Massachusetts, he began dating someone else. He notified me of this by phone, hinting they were taking overnight trips together. Then he stated he had decided to continue at M.I.T. rather than go to Stanford. I was dumbfounded. I assumed that was the end but didn't know fully until that Christmas. He sent me a Snoopy calendar and sent my mother two matched squirrel pins. A calendar? *I* was the one who collected animal pins. After that, things just faded away. Since we never had a big blow out about it, I guess one could say it was an amicable enough parting.

Needless to say, I was surprised to hear from him but acceded to inviting him over anyway. When he arrived, he had his Boston Bulldog named "Edison" in tow. He hadn't said a word about bringing him. Oh, crap! The dog barked and barked snappishly, the sound scraping raw the surface of my brain. Faust, who had been languishing on the sofa in the living room, whipped to attention. One look at this "inferior being" which was an intruder in his kingdom sent him into leaping onto the back of the rust-colored Naugahyde sofa. His back was arched. His gray fur stood on end. He hissed loudly. I silently rued the fact that it was too hot outside to have Danny lock Edison into his tan VW Beetle. Although, as the dog continued to bark and Faust continue to hiss and growl, it was rapidly becoming clear that my first impulse about dealing with the dog wouldn't have been such a bad idea after all. Tee hee.

Like all brachycephalic dogs, Edison's pushed in face and extremely short nose anatomically plagued him with respiratory problems. Just breathing normally was one. You would always know Edison was around because of the disconcerting sound of snuffling. That sound, no matter from animal or human, was guaranteed to make my stomach flip.

All I could envision was some man choosing not to blow his nose, instead snorting to rattle mucus in his nasal passages with the goal of transporting the viscous glob to his mouth in order to hurl it victoriously to the ground. Just the thought squeezed my throat and filled my mouth with saliva preparatory to vomiting.

We started to move toward the living room. However, as Faust began to switch his tail hard against the front window, making a loud thumping sound, I made a point of redirecting Danny back to my office. I tried to ignore Edison's snuffling as he strained his leash, choking himself, to move around the room to explore. I was just about to have us sit down when Edison crept up behind me, clasped my left calf, and began doing a vigorous polka against it, snorting loudly. In response, I began violently shaking my leg, trying to disengage him. But eyes glazed, he held me fast.

"Get off me, you disgusting creature!" How he could maintain his pogo-stick action even when hanging in the air boggled my mind. Danny was talking loudly to him, reprimanding him, pulling on his leash. I shouted, "Don't just talk to him!" My voice rose an octave, "Get him the hell off me."

Danny looked bewildered as to how to successfully make that happen. I was tempted to swing my leg widely sideways with a jerk and fling him into the wall. But as a respecter of animal-kind, I didn't want to severely injure him for being naturally repulsive. I just wanted to interrupt his joyously hyper-sexual focus. "Colonel Bat Guano" in *Dr. Strangelove* would have referred to it more explicitly as his "pre-version."

In the meantime, Faust was no longer hissing and growling. He had jumped off the sofa and had hurtled himself into the office, screaming, his vampire fangs exposed. Any moment he was going to hurl himself onto this obscene gyrating animal, employ his talons to detach Edison from my leg, and tear him apart, foreleg from haunch. There was only so much a cat could tolerate from canines, but this dog's uncouthness was beyond the pale. And it was attacking Faust's best bud?

While Edison was still trying to hang on, his dewclaws were raking bloody strips in my calf and shin as gravity made him slide down to a bowing position on the floor. I grabbed his paws, thrust them aside, and hustled Danny and Edison outside, quickly shutting the front door behind us. Faust loudly screamed again, despite his impaired lungs. We gravitated into the backyard where I had placed lawn chairs in the shade near the dining room. It had been only a matter of seconds before Faust would have bathed the hardwood floor with Edison's blood. This was a cat who normally got along with everyone. That didn't necessarily include dogs, especially this uncivilized one.

As soon as I closed the door, Faust dashed around to all the windows to see where we had gone. I looked toward the dining room windows and saw him, first at the windows at the front side of the house and then at those that faced the backyard. He glared, his mouth open, eyes large and wild, as he tried to crawl up the window pane. The glass didn't block his outraged comments.

Why had Danny come by? Years before I had taken about fifteen eight-by-ten photos of his parents and his dog in all kinds of settings for a portrait I was going to paint as a gift. At that time, I was often doing portraits in oil or ink as presents. I had already done one of Danny in oil for the Christmas before I moved to San Diego. Since we broke up, I didn't do the one of his parents and Edison. What Danny wanted was the photos. That was fine. I didn't want or need them. I wondered why he hadn't simply asked me to send them to him. Because I had them squirreled away in a carton with other photos of my family and Faust, they were easy to find. Then he let it slip that he and his girlfriend of x-number of years ago, whom he finally married, were now pfft. Was the light dawning? "Oh really," I responded, wanting to yawn. I immediately dropped the news into my short-term memory's circular file.

By the time I had sent Danny and his deviant "creature" on their way and re-entered the house, Faust had apparently forgiven me for not allowing him to dispatch Edison then and there. I was sure in his calculations there was always a next time. He stood on his hind legs and walked toward me. He sniffed the dried blood that had trickled down my left leg from Edison's dew claws. Smiling, I led him to the kitchen where I handed him his well-deserved kitty treat and cleaned up my wounds.

I had just been the victim of a canine sexual assault, which was not as frightening and vile as when I nearly had had my shoulder dislocated by someone who "knew" I really wanted sex because of what I had innocently done when I had last danced with him. In San Diego I had met Dave casually at monthly dances at the El Cortez hotel. Since he and I both liked to ballroom dance, we began to practice long and hard to enter an upcoming dance competition. After a particularly long, arduous session when we were working on the cha cha cha, to make it as legitimately Cuban as possible, I gave him a glancing kiss on his cheek, saying, "That was a great practice. I think we're nearly ready."

Though we had never dated, he chose to interpret that cheek peck as a come-on. We were in his car to drive me home, because my mother had to use our car. He started to maul me. I was thunder-struck. I started shouting, "Stop!" In spite of my adrenaline-surging, physical struggling and repeatedly screaming "NO!" he wanted to believe that the momentary graze of my lips superseded everything else. He'd taken one too many dips in the pool of *Playboy* philosophy about how females allegedly secretly communicated their untamed lust for males. As I managed to push him against the driver's door, he paused to proclaim self-righteously, "You were teasing me because you wanted it." Jeez, pal, you never thought to ask? Get a life!

Or the time I was literally kidnapped and held for over twenty-four hours by a psychotic dental professional who said, "I can make you love me. Tomorrow morning we'll pack up my motorcycle 'Sexy Sarah' and ride to Colorado where we'll live in a cabin in the mountains and raise chickens." Thankfully, despite my panic, I was able to bore him into near-unconsciousness by calmly and clinically talking him out of raping me. By the next morning when he plugged in the phones again and unlocked the doors, he had resumed his "normal" demeanor and happily returned me to my car, stating he was "looking forward to our next 'date'." Sexual assaults, even from dogs, get seared into your brain ... forever.

Which reminded me, if Danny ever visited again, though I didn't know why he would bother since I gave him no encouragement, he would *not* be bringing Edison. In the eventuality that he did, Faust wasn't going to let Edison off easy next time. To paraphrase Shakespeare, "Though he but little, he is fierce." He was ready, willing and able to make the dog suffer significant veterinary consequences. I suspect it likely would be something along the lines of what paid assassins are said to refer to as "wet work."

7

DRACULA RISES AGAIN

As our first Halloween approached in our new house, I dug out Faust's Dracula costume from a box in the basement. He and the children on Willow Road in Sudbury had enjoyed the holiday together. When I opened the front door there, Faust was waiting for them in his large orange plastic pumpkin which was planted on a high stool. Wearing his black mask and high-collared red cape with his vampire grin in place, he would pop up. Boo! His performance always triggered screams and giggles of delight.

This year I hung ghosts and skeletons outside near the lighted stoop to entice them since the house had been unoccupied for quite a while before I rented it. They arrived in dribs and drabs, mostly with their parents standing on the street awaiting them. The street had many houses. It was well lighted. The traffic was infrequent and slow. This made it an ideal place for children from all around the neighborhood to trick-or-treat.

When they rang the doorbell, I had the door swing open slowly. Unfortunately, it was without the requisite heavy, scary creak. Before them was Faust's large pumpkin on a stool facing them. On my cue he suddenly stood up. As expected, they shrieked, laughed nervously, and then started to pet him. Faust once again soaked up all the children's adoration. It had been a while since he had captured an audience's attention and was basking in the glory of it all. I had positioned a large L.L. Bean canvas tote bag filled with plastic bags of popcorn next to the door which I handed them out to them.

Knowing the children would likely be up to their elbows in candy, I had made air-popped popcorn for them, trying hard not to "sample" it all before they arrived. I had made it without oil so it wouldn't get soggy before they reached home. They could then add butter and salt to taste. Maybe it could help take the edge off all the sweets they would have practically inhaled from their begging for Halloween "alms."

Even though he couldn't wait to get out of his costume, Faust stalwartly stayed in character even with his mask askew, revealing only one eye, from his upward thrusts, until the last straggler departed. Then he sat quietly in his pumpkin, pawing my arm to finally remove his now-annoying apparel. Maybe next year I ought to make him a different costume. Maybe an "Edison" dog suit, I malevolently snickered to myself. "That's bad. So bad! I couldn't do that to him."

It was fun seeing the varied costumes the children wore.

Some were slap-dash ones, like ghosts, and others were more intricate like super-heroes, princesses, and pirates. There were lots of duplicates, but a silver-suited spaceman stood out. It reminded me of my favorite 1951 science-fiction film, *The Day the Earth Stood Still*. Michael Rennie starred as Klaatu, the alien emissary who had arrived on Earth in his flying saucer to warn its leaders through a world-wide demonstration of power that they had to give up their war-like folly of atomic experimentation. It was he who spoke the famous line, "Klaatu barada nikto" to Gort, the gigantic military guardian master robot which protected Klaatu and piloted his intergalactic vehicle.

Decades after I had first seen the film as a child, I had found the 1940 short story on which it was loosely based, "Farewell to the Master" by Harry Bates. While I often hated the changes film makers tended to make to a film's original work that I liked, I had to applaud director Robert Wise's alterations. The film, however dated, is still a classic.

8

BECOMING KNOWN

As business increased, I was asked if I wanted to join the American Cancer Society Charles River Chapter as their public relations person. In that position, I created cancer- and ACS-relevant articles for the *Wellesley Townsman* newspaper and public service announcement (PSA) videos. One PSA, for example, was "Road to Recovery." It was about encouraging people to volunteer to drive cancer patients to treatment or help coordinate transportation for them. The video we did showed how a driver arrived at the patient's home, made sure the patient had everything she or he needed for their treatment, then drove them as a friend to the hospital where the treatment was taking place then picked them up afterward to drive them home again.

As director, I tried to make sure those who participated in the video were a diverse group so everyone was represented. I was the first person to involve a young Africa-American woman to play the doctor who greeted the patient coming for chemotherapy. As I later understood it, this was not appreciated by some elder white-to-the-bone residents of affluent Wellesley. My feeling was, "That's just too bad."

Faust participated in the three PSAs I did. In the "Road to Recovery" he sat quietly in the back seat of the car while I drove, conversing with the patient in the passenger seat. I wanted to have him sit on the patient's lap but deep-sixed the idea because I was given to understand ACS might not have found it acceptable or fitting: "off-putting" was how it was expressed to me. In "Reach to Recovery" where cancer survivors talk with others recently diagnosed with cancer, Faust sat comfortingly with the survivor during the interview. The third PSA was for "Making Strides for Breast Cancer Walks" where Faust wore a pink harness and walked with the volunteers.

The articles I wrote highlighted ACS events, new programs, important cancer research, new diagnostic testing protocols, multi-specialty hospital cancer programs, cancer preventive care, controversial topics like radical mastectomies, range of reconstructive surgeries, the psychological, emotional, sociological, and physical aspects of dealing with cancer as told by present and former cancer sufferers. I also dealt with the significant clinical and psychological benefits of pet therapy. I used Faust as an example of what an animal can do to relieve an ill person's stress, lower blood pressure, lighten his or her depression, and give them motivation to fight.

As a result of my work with ACS, I began to freelance for

the Wellesley newspaper, writing science- and business-based articles using many local professionals and business people. For example, I interviewed Dana Young about time management; Roger and Nancy Pelissier about portrait photography; Gloria and Don White about Shaklee; Susan and Richard Reardon about organizational and management development; Betsy and Karl Baumann about financial planning. I even interviewed Faust for an article on the need to test cats for feline leukemia.

As part of my work on mentoring and networking, I had created The Mentoring Network, which consisted of five different but interrelated services out of the networking and mentoring seminars I was doing. These reflected ways people could connect with others to advance in their jobs, careers, or businesses. Then I began seeking speaking engagements covering alternative ways to promote oneself to get jobs as well as using mentors and networking which I had spelled out in my first book, *Create Your Own Career Opportunities: A Proven Program for Systematically Developing Behavioral Strategies to Achieve Job and Career Goals.*

Some of the places I made presentations included Boston College, Wellesley College, Simmons College, Lesley College, Suffolk University, Merrill Lynch, Honeywell Bull, Maine Career Educational Consortium, Boston Center for Adult Education, Greater Boston Chamber of Commerce, Rotary Clubs, and the Commonwealth of Massachusetts Department of Professional Education and Training. Faust joined in wherever he was allowed—which wasn't at the Rotary.

Just before Faust and I were leaving for the Maine Career Educational presentation, I discovered to my horror that the suit I was going to wear was too tight. I wouldn't dare bend over even slightly. I could imagine the torturous sound of pants' fabric detaching itself from its back seam as I folded myself into the car. Crap! I needed a new wardrobe until I shed the extra weight I had gained as I babied a knee problem that resulted from my running forty-plus miles a week. Time was whipping by as I searched for something appropriate to wear.

What I finally found was a pair of white slacks, a white long-sleeve blouse, and an open-front red-and-white check vest that breathed with me. It was definitely *not* the look I'd striven for but at least I was clothed and not at risk of being exposed privately in public. Faust seemed to approve. I had planned to leave Faust behind because the organizers said they couldn't, or wouldn't, accommodate him. Fine. He wasn't their problem. He would stay with *me* anyway while I ran my workshop.

After a several-hour uneventful drive, Faust and I found the classroom where participants were beginning to congregate. I'd parked Faust's open carrier on a desk behind me where I had a pile of handouts. Just as I was literally about to start my presentation, one of the event organizers rushed into the room. All out of breath, she exclaimed, "There's been a scheduling problem. You have to make your two-hour workshop into an hour program."

Whoa, dude! An *hour*? That torpedoed the participation part of the program. Standing in front of the assembled, I had to, on the spur of the moment, choose what lecture material and exercises to use and how to employ them. I heard movement in Faust's carrier and looked back. He looked concerned, stretching his neck to see what was going on. Turning to him, I whispered in his ear that if he were good, he could do his dance for the assembled. He looked relieved. This was going to be an interesting "workshop"!

Overall, it went all right, I guess. My tongue didn't disconnect from my brain but I wasn't happy with my presentation. The instant restructuring rendered it, to my mind, less linear, comprehensive, and smooth than I had originally organized it. This was a big disappointment to me because it could have been so much more informative and fun if it had gone on as scheduled. Of course, the participants had had no idea what I had planned to say, so they may not have been as disappointed as I was. I never discovered what the problem had been. I did wonder if anyone else's program had suffered from this awkward "re-scheduling."

At the end of the hour as I provided relevant handouts and an evaluation sheet, I invited Faust to dance. He climbed out of his carrier and tripped the light fantastic on the desk, before sitting, waiting for acclaim, with his self-satisfied grin. His prancing elicited smiles, chuckles, and murmurs.

I was pleased that most evaluations were positive and referred to the usefulness of the subject matter. But, of course, there was ONE that didn't. There's always "one." Naturally, *that* was the one I remembered most. All it stated was, "You didn't look business-like or professional. And you brought a CAT?"

"Good grief! 'Miss Manners.' I had hoped you would have gotten more out of that busy, jam-packed hour than just that."

I was especially pleased to receive a call from the Greater Boston Chamber of Commerce which wanted me to speak at their big annual convention. I was to be on a panel discussing how to effectively create job, career, and business opportunities, speaking specifically on the unpublicized use of networking and mentors. Of course, I said "yes" … until they called back.

This second person said there was a problem. "In order for you to speak at the convention, you have to be a member of the GBCC. That would be a fee of $100. Furthermore, you would need to purchase a ticket for the convention and that was $75."

I was aghast. I said, "Let me get this straight. You not only want me to speak at your convention for *free* but also want to *charge* me to do so? I don't think so."

Sounding flustered, apparently not expecting my response, she asked me to hold so she could check on it. After five minutes of my fingers drumming, like Gene Krupa belting out "Big Noise from Winnetka," she returned, "We've never done this before but we're going to make a big exception for you. You don't have to become a member. We'll only charge you for the ticket."

"Wait a second. You invited me to participate, I assumed, as your guest," I responded. "If you're now taking back the invitation, I guess your panel will a person short and networking and mentors won't be covered. That can work for me."

"No, no, no," she replied, sounding, flustered. "Just another moment." She disappeared but returned more quickly than last time. "Of course, we'd like you to participate as our *guest*."

I participated without Faust because of the noise and chaos at the convention center. I shared a lot of info and resources and had fun. Furthermore, the gig didn't hurt my visibility and credibility either. And no, I never joined the GBCC. Their peculiar behavior had not spoken well of their savvy from a public relations' perspective. And when I arrived home, Faust at least hadn't cleared the counters to show his displeasure at having been left behind. Besides, he'd already pulled that prank. He generally chose not to repeat himself. He was more creative than that.

9

GONE IN A PUFF OF SMOKE

As the months rolled by, the house and business were coming along. Faust was using the gnarled apple tree which grew in front of the six-foot-tall rock ledge, to which a tall mountain ash clung precariously, for his Flying Wallendas practice. To take breaks from business I had started working in the yard, mostly to clean out around perennials and shrubs as he practiced. Then one Saturday while I was mowing the grass, I heard the phone. Rushing into the house, I discovered it was from John whom I had known years ago from my time at M.I.T. and had dated for three months. I was astonished to hear from him, especially given our last, less than good-natured, encounter. This afternoon he and his fourteen-year-old son were passing through on their way back from their hiking trip to the Pemigewasset Wilderness. This was the 45,000-acre federally designated wilderness area in the heart of New Hampshire's White Mountains. He wanted to stop by. Not thrilled, I couldn't imagine why but acceded.

Meeting and interacting with his then ten-year-old son was

one of the most obnoxious experiences I had ever had. As a result, John and I had parted company. I did not look forward to repeating it. Given the circumstances, the intervening four years were highly unlikely to have changed anything very much for the better, at least not without heavy-duty therapeutic intervention for both of them.

Before Faust came into my life, John, his son, J.P., and I had driven to D.C. late on a Friday to take in the sites over the weekend. When we arrived, his father asked J.P., "Since you've been so excited about seeing the National Air and Space Museum, would you like to go there first?"

"No," J.P. responded petulantly. "I didn't want to come on this trip with HER (elegantly referring to me). I told her and she threatened me. She said I had to pretend I was really excited or else. I was scared. I wanted to tell you but I was afraid to. I didn't know what she'd do to me." Then he glared at me with his lying eyes and said, as a small smirk graced his lips, "You've ruined everything. I hate you for it."

John looked at me, jaw dropping, eyebrows shooting upward, shocked. I looked him in the eye and said, "Nope. It never happened. Not a single word of it." Then I turned to J.P. and asked, "Why are you saying these untrue things?"

His eyes widened, looking like a subject in a Kean painting, his lower lip quivering with a tear glistening, ready to drop dramatically. "I don't lie!" he said with indignation. "You know it's true. You're so mean to me when Dad's not looking.

She's lying, Dad. You know I wouldn't lie to you."

John stammered, instantly furious, "Are calling my son a liar?"

I wanted to say, "You bet your sweet cheeks, Daddy, I am." Instead, I tried to explain. "It looks to me that J.P. is playing some game—maybe out of jealousy or fear—to set us against one another." As you might imagine, that did not go over well. I was thinking about Eric Berne's *Games People Play* and Everett Shostrom's *Man, The Manipulator* while John was taking off his Clark Kent glasses in a phone booth, readying himself to protect mom, apple pie, and the American way—but most especially his "victimized" son.

John looked incensed, insulted, and disbelieving. "How dare you impugn J.P.! Children don't lie and they don't 'play games.' J.P. would never do that even if he could."

I didn't know how much of John's argument was from gross ignorance or self-protective denial or both. Of course, even much, much younger children lie and play games. Remember the behavior of two-year-olds? I considered both snappy and clinical responses but figured it was smarter to bury them. I said simply, "Not true."

That was how the D.C. experience began and it didn't get any better. For the rest of our weekend, J.P. negotiated every aspect of what we were doing. He continually made nasty references to me. When I objected, he'd roll his eyes, sigh, and shake his head, stating it was only a joke. He never expressed responsibility for or regret about anything he did. He was always the poor, down-trodden victim. Boo hoo. Of course, his father never said anything. When J.P. promised to do the slightest thing for me, like tell his father I had gone to use the nearby restroom, he never kept his promises. Instead, he blamed me for having "left him all alone," stating, "I was afraid she wasn't coming back." Intermittently, he was reinforcing the notion that I was purposely terrorizing him.

In general, I tried to keep my mouth shut. However, when I felt it was serious enough to respond to his most egregious actions against me, like when he unquestionably grabbed my breast, I remained calm and fact-oriented as I tried to establish some boundaries. J.P., of course, acted totally offended, denied everything, "I didn't! Why are you lying about me?" He sought out his father's protection from this unwarranted "attack."

As a result, John once again became angry with me, seemingly unable to accept the remotest possibility of any untoward behavior from his son. I was the liar, the instigator, spreading falsehoods and discord any chance I got. Consequently, he was irritated and on edge with me most of the trip. I wasn't exactly delighted that he never once instructed his son about what was appropriate or inappropriate or imposed any discipline.

This kid at ten was already a classic manipulator and controller: sneaky, lying, and devious. He was well on his way to being entrenched in these negative behaviors in adulthood and a life of unhealthy social functioning, unless he received lots of therapy. "Therapy? How dare you!" Needless to say, after that, John and I stopped dating by mutual consent.

When John and now 14-year-old J.P. arrived, I viewed them with a jaundiced eye. While John and I would be engaged in conversation in the living room, J.P. was stationed in the dining room, with a glass of lemonade and chocolate chip cookies I'd made, where I had set up the TV and VCR with some available action videos. I was flabbergasted that John had even contemplated coming by. We hadn't communicated in any way since D.C. I couldn't figure out what his motive might be. But over coffee, he haltingly stated, "I think we should try again." I nearly swallowed my tongue. Really? I thought. You surely must be kidding! You're a walking disaster. I'd rather slather my naked body with honey and lie on a fire ant hill.

Faust, who had been snuggled on my lap, jumped down to wander into the dining room to see what was going on in there. A little later J.P. called about needing to use the bathroom. "At the top of the stairs," I directed.

Ten minutes later I heard a scuffle, claws scratching the wood floor, and a loud mohw. What? Where? I jumped off the sofa, quickly looked around the first floor, then leapt up the stairs. J.P. was sitting on the top step looking innocent. I called to Faust. He invariably would come to me when I called. After all, he knew he'd likely get a tasty treat, a luxurious full-body scratch, or play time as a reward for responding. I didn't see or hear him anywhere.

I asked J.P., "Where's the cat?"

Wearing his blameless look, he shrugged his shoulders and said, "I don't know."

What? The cat magically disappeared? He de-materialized in a puff of smoke? I looked at him squarely in the eyes and knew the little son of a bitch was lying. My heart started to cannonade. What had he done with Faust? Glaring at him, I thought, you little bastard, you better not have hurt him or I guarantee I will rain such hell down upon you.

I checked the bathroom clothes hamper and shower. No. Swallowing hard, I even lifted the toilet lid to check the bowl. It was Faust-less. Thank goodness! Then I opened the linen closet. No. I kept calling. At the end of the hall I checked the room where I stored all my books and papers. I opened filing cabinet drawers. No. The closet. No. Calling, I hoped he would respond ... *if he could.*

It was then I heard a tiny, muffled mohw-like sound. But I still couldn't locate its direction. My blood pressure was likely off the clinical chart. In my bedroom I frantically checked under the bed. No. In my dresser drawers. No. In my clothes closet. No. "Faust," I shouted, a note of increasing panic in my voice.

As I entered the second bedroom at head of the stairs, I caught something in my peripheral vision. "Oh, my God!" I gasped. There to the left on the narrow sill outside the locked window overlooking the backyard was a confused, frightened cat, barely keeping his balance. His face was flattened against the glass, his pupils dilated, nervously seeking out his mom. This was the only window in the house which currently was missing a screen. When he saw me, he became excited. His body started to jiggle. But in doing so, he was putting himself in jeopardy. Damn! Damn! Damn!

As I unlocked the window, I slowly started to raise it. I was talking softly to him, hoping he'd relax a little. Maybe he would lessen his frantic pressure against the glass. If he maintained it, when the wooden rail of the window reached his head, it would likely push him back. As soon as I could, I stuck my fingers out underneath it. He immediately lowered his head to happily lick my fingers. Ever the feline acrobat extraordinaire, he still somehow maintained his balance. Hurrah! This allowed me to raise the window enough to quickly grab him.

As I cuddled him in my arms to comfort him, my heart was still pounding like artillery bombardment. Then I heard footsteps behind me. J.P. was now watching and his father was standing behind him. I looked at the teenager with a mother tiger's fury I was disinclined to cover. I wanted to smash him in his face and shout at him, "You little fucker, get the hell out of my house before I kill you!"

Instead, as was expected of me as a psychology professional, I swallowed enough of my rage to inquire in a strained voice, "Why did you put Faust outside on the window ledge? You scared him. He might have fallen and died. Is that why you did it? To scare him? To see if he'd die?"

John interceded, "You can't just accuse him."

J.P. said, "I didn't do anything."

Ignoring John and still directed at J.P., I continued, "You can say that all you'd like but *you* did it." To both of them I stated, with my anger now barely under control, "One. The cat didn't open a locked window. Two. He didn't step outside on this narrow ledge. Three. He didn't then close the window behind him. Four. He didn't lock it from the *inside*. Yes, I can accuse him!"

John looked distressed and confused. He faced his son and asked his son, "Did you do that?"

I rolled my eyes in exasperation. I thought for heaven's sake don't ask him that. Of course, he'll say he didn't. Jeez, John, it isn't necessary for him to confess to you for you to address the situation. This kid will lie about his misdeeds no matter how much incontrovertible evidence there is against him. Remember when he stabbed big holes in my Monstera, my Swiss cheese plant's leaves, with a pair of scissors?

"This situation is totally unacceptable," I seethed. "John, You can choose to disbelieve the obvious or not. Either way, it's time for you two to leave ... NOW!"

Part of me wanted to read John the riot act. He needed to tell his son that what he'd done was not only inappropriate but unsupportable. He needed to discipline him by choosing a suitable punishment. But I could tell John wouldn't do any of these things. From our conversation only minutes before, I had learned that his ex-wife still had custody—not that John could care for his son full-time with his work schedule—so John was allowed to see his son every three months for a week. He knew his son blamed him for the divorce. Guilt was undoubtedly why he was always kowtowing to him, acceding to whatever the child demanded, no matter the immediate or ultimate cost to himself, anyone else like me, or J.P.

Over our short time together in the past, I had repeatedly seen John try to buy his son's affection by calling him from wherever we were, no matter how inconvenient it was for me. We often had to wait hours to do anything we'd planned until he could reach his son first. One time he even interrupted our outing to drive around a rural area aimlessly to find a pay phone. Then upon finding one, he left me sitting in his car in the baking hot sun while he called his son. Where was his concern for me? Where was his respect for me? During our D.C. trip, I had seen the full display of J.P. getting away with outrageous behaviors. With John not addressing them, he was inadvertently reinforcing them.

Consequently, J.P. manipulated and controlled his father and was never made responsible for his actions much less disciplined for them by his father. It seemed sad to me that John's guilt-based reluctance to shape up and start acting like a *real* father, giving necessary structure, limits, boundaries, and what was expected of his son (or any person) participating in a civil society, had already helped set J.P.'s downward spiraling direction in concrete.

Their relationship was like a pond of quicksand. While you may not drown, you may be trapped indefinitely until external help can pull you out. I had unknowingly dipped my toe into it once before but wasn't masochistic enough to take a flying leap into it again. That was the end of that visit … and any future visits. John never had a prayer of our ever getting back together before this day. Furthermore, the Faust situation just wrote it across the sky in neon letters fifty feet high. Still hugging Faust with a feeling of lingering alarm, I reiterated, as strongly and clearly as possible, that they should high-tail it … ASAP … and *never* darken my door again.

After they left and I locked up, I felt my fear-tightened shoulder muscles beginning to spasm. It was the right moment to take a hot bath. I rarely took baths, preferring showers, but Faust preferred my taking baths. As I settled into the steaming tub with a little Chanel No. 5 bath oil, Faust sauntered into the bathroom. Suddenly he jumped onto the rim of the tub. To my surprise and joy he began to walk along the edge and serenade me with his scratchy feline version of what I assumed was "Che gelida manina." His mimicking what Rodolfo sings sweetly to Mimi in *La Bohème* at their meeting when her candle goes out on the stairs seemed so apropos. Faust hadn't done that since our first year together in Sudbury. I think he was telling me that he was going to be okay. I needed that reassurance.

10

MENTORING

One service of The Mentoring Network was a Networking Reception. Participants paid a minimal fee to meet and be matched with those who had information or skills they wanted. That turned out to be a bad business move since this had to be a low-volume event, no more than twenty people. To be profitable it required many more participants. But large numbers of participants would have made what I had to do impossible because this was hands-on and individualized. As participants entered, I asked each of them what skills or information they had to offer and what they wanted to come away with. Then I introduced each person to those who had those skills or information. It was an exhausting, red-ink evening of mixing and matching.

Faust usually attended, sometimes sitting in his open carrier or on a gray steel folding chair near the refreshments. Since he had his own canned salmon, he rarely checked out the pastry goodies set out on the table. He wasn't a pastry aficionado anyway. Well, there was *one* time. One of my networking facilitators, Ella, had brought a pink pastry box with her. Initially I assumed that the contents were for the reception but wondered why she hadn't put it out yet. I thought I'd do it for her but then stopped. Maybe I was wrong. I shouldn't just assume and then blithely act on the assumption as if it were valid. That could be very awkward if I were wrong. Of course, I could ask but that didn't occur to me as people slowly began to arrive. Ella left the room to make copies of some networking resources I was going to hand out. I surreptitiously sneaked a peek while she was gone. The box contained a tantalizing pineapple upside down cake. Hard to say if this was to be tonight's donation. Before she could return, I simply closed the lid and went back to greeting guests.

Apparently, Faust had seen me and was likewise curious about what was in the box. Copying my actions was one of the ways he'd learned his new behaviors. As I was making notes on each of the guest's desires, he hopped onto the table, crept across it, adeptly winding his way around the food, napkins, plastic utensils, punch bowl, paper plates, and cups. When he reached the box, he lifted his right paw to push up on the edge of the lid. I had unintentionally left a sixteenth of an inch opening so he gained purchase. In my peripheral vision, I saw him stick his nose at the opening, sniff, and then slide his right paw over the cardboard lip in toward the cake.

Oh, damn! I didn't want to do anything to startle him which might send the box and its contents smashing on to the floor. Instead, I said his name quietly but sharply. He stopped, looked up at me. As I gestured him back with my freehand, he slowly retreated backwards, carefully missing what was behind him. I hurried to the table and closed the lid again just as Ella returned. Regaining my composure, I pointed to the box and said, "In case that's not for here, you might want to put that someplace safe."

"Oh, yeah, thanks," she replied. "I'm taking it to a friend after the reception. I'll put it with my purse on the floor behind the table." Whew! I had lucked out.

One of the problems I occasionally encountered with some new members of The Mentoring Network was that they expected to get positive results immediately. They would bewail the fact that things had not changed for the better fast enough. This desire for instant gratification occasionally obstructed the processes I was having them follow. This was especially difficult in cultivating networking, or any, relationships where both were expected to give, which took time.

Consequently, it is too easy for some people to drop ideas, plans, projects, or relationships if things didn't go their way or meet their expectations immediately, ultimately leaving them disappointed and frustrated. What always came to mind as an example of "don't give up too soon" was how Edison and his development team were trying to make the previously-existing light bulb into an economical, practical, and safe incandescent electric light through a viable system of lighting (including generators, cables, and meters). After 1,999 failures, they finally discovered a type of filament—carbonized sewing thread— that would work. Success was built on time, effort, and a foundation of informative failures.

Even Ella had expressed the desire for instant gratification, but in a slightly different context. She was very fond of Faust, giving him a chuck under the chin whenever she was saw him. She stated that she was envious of our relationship and had, as a result, been considering adding a cat to her life. As a result, she visited the local animal rescue shelter where she had found a hip-disabled cat she was drawn to. But like so many other people she tended to be impatient.

Soon thereafter she told me, "I'm thinking of taking the cat back. We haven't bonded. I wanted her to be my best friend but it hasn't happened."

"How long have you had her?"

"Two days," she replied.

"Would you expect to bond with a human stranger after only two days?"

"Well, no."

"It's the same thing. You need to give her more time. It's all new to her too. She's testing the waters, as you are, to see if you likewise meet *her* expectations of a new best friend. You need to show her that you really care, that she's protected and safe, that she can trust you, and that she now has a permanent, loving home. She has to have a sense that you'll always be there for her. You know that Faust and I weren't instantaneous best friends. Our close relationship developed over lots of time. Give her at least two weeks. Interact with her as much as you can in the interim. Have fun. Show affection. You know that worthwhile relationships of any kind take weeks if not months and more. I'll bet you'll see a big difference soon."

And she did. Within ten days she called me to tell me, "Katy-O is the very best cat. She even sleeps on my pillow with me. We're already best buds. I can't believe I was going to take her back. Thanks."

In addition to the Networking Receptions, The Mentoring Network Program included an abilities-assessment consulting service, computer matching of individuals who had what others wanted or had discovered they needed, as well as a monthly newsletter with articles, tips, and advice, and seminars for organizational education, social effectiveness, anxiety management, interpersonal communication, impression management, and career development. All this was for membership at $144 per year. However, one could attend the Networking Receptions without being a member. It was a way to personally introduce all the services to as many people as possible.

While most Networking Receptions were very predictable, one turned out to be like an episode from the "Twilight Zone." This one was held in the Psychology Building at Boston

University in a large room on the ground floor. The crowd was three times the size of normal attendance which kept Faust lurking in his carrier most of the evening, sticking his head out occasionally for a pet. The numbers were great for interest but not for facilitating connections. I usually held the receptions at M.I.T. in the Alfred P. Sloan Building which was readily available to me but had a problem with elevator access for the disabled. The elevator ran to just below the floor I was on, leaving everyone having to climb ten stairs to attend. That was awkward and I felt guilty and embarrassed about it. My excuse was that finding free space was nearly impossible in Boston or Cambridge so I took whatever I could find. So much for conforming to the dictates of the Americans with Disabilities Act and compassionately assisting the disabled to participate.

For this reception at B.U. I had invited a locally-known Cambridge business consultant who had written a book on time management. From our telephone conversations I thought we might network and work together in some way since we did similar things. I had suggested that at the reception while she could answer reception participants' business questions, she could also get some clients from this diverse business-oriented group. It seemed like a win-win to me.

How wrong could I have been! No sooner had she made an entrance and observed the assemblage than she said knowingly, "You invited me merely to impress the other participants."

That astonished me. Was she kidding? I didn't see people running up to her, oohing and ahing, or genuflecting in reverence. No one approached her to get her autograph. She wasn't a Peter Drucker, Stephen Covey, Tom Peters, or Dale Carnegie. If she was a legend, it was, apparently, only in her own mind. In fact, I had had no reason to believe she was even considered a "celebrity," that people outside of a select group in Cambridge would know her, except for her one book which had been published many years previously.

As people approached me, I introduced her, her book, and her consulting business. Participants seemed to take her at face value. I didn't notice any signs of recognition of her face or name. As I explained to her in detail how The Mentoring Network worked, and how the different services dovetailed upon one another, she stopped me.

Looking over the large group, she smugly shook her head. "Firstly, I don't believe you have that many members for your program." I started to reply but she cut me off. "Secondly," she swept the room with her hand, "this isn't my level of client. I don't see our networking or working together." We were standing near the front table where the refreshments and Faust were placed. Faust started to lean out of his carrier toward her, as if to grab her arm with his claws exposed. Fortunately, he missed. If he'd snagged her, she probably would have sued me.

She sounded as if her *real* fans, the chosen, enlightened, high-paying ones, were all waiting with bated breath elsewhere for her return. Because *they* had passed her critical evaluation, she allowed them to be bathed in her brilliant business consulting insights. She exited stage left shortly after her dramatic pronouncement. Alas, no one at the gathering seemed to notice but Faust, who no doubt thought he had provoked it to his apparent gratification.

11

JOINING THE BOSTON MARATHON

The third Monday of April was Patriot's Day and the annual running of the Boston Marathon. Covering twenty-six miles and three hundred and eighty-five yards, the race began in Hopkinton, west-southwest of Boston along Rt. 135, included hilly and flat terrain, and ended in Copley Square in Boston, near the Boston Public Library. It ran east through Ashland, Framingham, Natick, *and* Wellesley before it went on to Newton Lower Falls then Boston. Faust and I were definitely going to perch ourselves on the highway guardrail across from Wellesley College to watch the runners pour through Wellesley. I had dreamed of participating but never progressed beyond doing a paltry eight miles a day. This race's endurance required more distance work than I put in.

Faust was in his harness and leash but I had on his knapsack just in case. Every so often a runner would swing near enough to Faust when he was in my arms to pat him on his head. He reveled in the attention which I'm sure he felt he deserved. As he watched the onslaught of runners, he became excited, leaping out of my arms to try to balance on the guardrail beside me. When I wasn't focused on him as I watched the runners, he jumped down, crept to the edge of the asphalt, and sneakily slunk forward onto the road.

What everyone was waiting for was the perennial favorite, Team Hoyt. That was triathlon athlete Dick Hoyt and his cerebral palsy-handicapped son Rick whom he pushed in a Running Chair. They had begun to "run" together in 1977 when Rick asked his father if they could run in a five-mile race to benefit a lacrosse player at his school who had become paralyzed. After that, they incredibly also participated in two hundred and fifty triathlons.

Faust was mesmerized by the Hoyts' unusual, customized Running Chair, which was produced especially for them by Southbridge Tool and Manufacturing. He even tried to catch it as it passed. If I hadn't spotted him and quickly pulled him back to the edge of the street again, he likely would have run right onto the wheeled chair. His actions likewise would have interfered with an upcoming blind runner who was being assisted on his right side by another runner. My heart did a flip. Fortunately, neither runner appeared to see or sense Faust so neither broke his stride. I quickly stuffed Faust into his knapsack, facing over my shoulder. I would have died of humiliation and self-reproach if we had interfered with any runner or disrupted the marathon. It was my very good luck that no police officer had witnessed Faust's—no, *my*—transgression. I would have been given a ticket which I truly would have deserved but I still would have died a thousand public deaths.

We had watched about half the runners when I checked my watch. Drat! I knew it was time to hurry home to catch the TV coverage of the lead runners putting on their final spurts of speed to cross the finish line first. Faust hated leaving Rt. 135. He kept looking around as runners streamed by.

By the time I was lifting my rear off the guardrail, he was struggling to pull himself out of the backpack. He obviously wanted to stay as long as possible, maybe until the very last runner cleared the half-way point. By now my hands were scarlet from clapping for everyone who passed—they all deserved recognition—but my right wrist was turning blue from the tightness of Faust's leash holding him back from escaping.

We rushed through the woods below Rt. 135, along Weston Road, to arrive back home just in time to see the male and female winners. Exhilarated, I thought that maybe one of these days I'd put in more time and distance to get myself prepared to join the marathon. But I'd have to qualify at another marathon first, maybe New York's, before I could apply to run in the Boston Marathon. This really was something that *could* possibly happen if I wanted it badly enough.

Team Hoyt was inspirational. Both Dick and Rick were motivated to prove that life goes on no matter what your disability might be. As Rick was quoted as saying, "Disability disappears when we're running. My dad is my hands and feet." Their vision always left me feeling very lucky and that someday, perhaps, I could accomplish some noble vision as well.

They always finished this race, that is until many years later when the two bombs exploded near the finish line in 2013. They had had about a mile to go when they and thousands of other participants who were still running the race were stopped by officials. Then, finally, after completing the Boston Marathon in 2014, they called it quits. To honor their decades of ingenious efforts for people with disabilities a bronze statue of them running together was installed on the front lawn of Center School in Hopkinton a few yards from the Marathon starting line. Very stirring and well deserved.

12

EMPATHY

As a five-year-old child living in Pennsylvania, I had so many earaches, strep throats, and ongoing pain that it seemed I was rarely well in the cooler months. After the last bacterial bout and before the next, I was finally scheduled to have my tonsils removed. Since at my tender age I hadn't a clue what that entailed, I had been told repeatedly prior to surgery what a rainbow-and-unicorn experience it would be: practically no pain, in and out in a day or two, to rejoice in no further strep throats, earaches, or tonsillitis. Life would be beautiful.

Because of my ignorance and child's trust the constant propaganda worked big time. I was truly excited about the upcoming procedure, skipping around the house, singing, "I'm going to have my tonsils out." On the day of days, I was so jazzed I told the surgeon as they wheeled me into the operating room that I couldn't wait. Happily, I even offered my profuse thanks for what he was about to do to me.

However, all that I had been told to reassure and comfort me was a cruel lie. After the fact, I wondered if my parents had known that. Were they deceiving me purposely? Didn't the truth matter to them? Hadn't they been informed? Or were they just unaware of what would take place? They obviously had no conception of its immediate effect on me. To be charitable, I'm sure things had changed since they had had their own tonsils out. But the whole incident left me feeling betrayed and less trusting of my parents' words to me. Now I was also cynical and skeptical about the statements of the medical establishment. When were they telling me the truth and when were they patronizing me, feeding me verbal pablum?

My post-op experience was horrific. NO PAIN?! My throat screamed in pain. Swallowing felt nearly impossible. Consequently, I thought I'd choke on the collecting saliva which began to seep out of the corners of my mouth until I could muster the courage to swallow. I was scared and trying not to cry because it hurt too much to make sounds in my throat. The saliva was riddled with blood because the bleeding from my wound was taking its time to subside. The only thing that challenged the pain was that I was thirsty and starving. I hadn't been allowed anything to eat or drink since 6 p.m. the day before. I hoped I'd have something soon, something soothing. I'd heard about being given ice cream after tonsillectomies to sooth the throat. That cold creaminess sounded good, especially the cold part. Maybe I could get that down. I desperately needed something to abate the pain but nothing was being provided so far as I could tell. I wanted to broadcast, "Help me! I'm in pain. And I'm bleeding too!"

I had to sit upright against an upended pillow because of my ongoing bloody seepage. Tears continued to silently stream down my crimson face. But everyone in white seemed to be ignoring me. I waved unsuccessfully to get someone's attention. Time passed. I needed help so badly. Panic had wrapped itself around my heart like a boa constrictor. I could barely breathe. A nurse finally came by some time in the afternoon to ask if I were ready for some food and drink. I carefully mouthed, "Yes!" I clasped my throat and pointed to mouth, barely whispering, "Hurts!" Even whispering hurt. She didn't respond. I didn't know if she hadn't heard me or chose to intentionally disregard me.

Time had no reference point. When she returned later, what she had brought totally astonished me. Where was my dish of ice cream? On a tray was a plate with a piece of dry toast cut in half and a glass of ginger ale. I didn't understand. Fear gripped me. "No ice cream?" I forced a whisper.

"No, we don't do that any longer. This is better for you."

I warily looked at the rough texture of the toast. I didn't believe her but I compliantly took her at her word, hoping my fear was unwarranted. Even though I was manufacturing saliva by the gallon, I didn't seem to be able to produce enough to moisten the small piece of toast I put in my mouth. I gingerly moved it around from one cheek to the other until I thought it might be saturated and ready to swallow. It wasn't. The scratchy toast scraped the collecting protective blood clots from the sutured incision in my raw throat. Reinvigorating the unquantifiable pain, it also started the wound bleeding profusely again. Blood clots and red liquid filled my mouth, dribbling down my chin. I tried to catch the nurse's attention. By the time she reappeared, about thirty minutes later, the bleeding had slowed but my lower face and chest were smeared red.

She looked at me as if I were a messy eater. Then she said, "Don't worry about it. It's just the body's cleaning process." Don't worry about it? I'm still bleeding. Maybe I was going to bleed to death!

While I'd have preferred to have had water which had no bubbles to pop on the angry, laid-bare flesh, the ginger ale eventually did have a slightly soothing effect. Maybe it was the sugar or the carbon dioxide. A little ice would have made it more helpful. Some half a century later I discovered that ginger can reduce the pain of inflammation but that was *real* ginger, not some late 40s' ginger-flavored syrup.

For two days I struggled with dry toast and ginger ale. Eventually the suture-scraping ceased to start more new blood flowing. I no longer felt faint, which was probably more from panic than from blood loss. But it didn't lessen the torment. If I had thought the earaches and strep were bad, there was no comparison to this. Because aspirin is acetylsalicylic acid, I couldn't even take that for pain without causing myself more burning pain as the flakes scorched the wound.

I couldn't believe it. The "joys" of tonsillectomy! I'd been sold on a ribbon-wrapped basket of kittens when in reality I had received a brown paper sack of steaming dog turds. As time went by and I'd finally recovered and could actually get some soothing ice cream, I consoled myself that at least I no longer had my tonsils and all that that had beneficently conferred upon me. Or so I had happily thought for years. But things are not always what they seem.

Many decades later in Wellesley when I suddenly developed a sore throat, I thought nothing of it. Pathogens of all kinds were always floating around where people gathered. Besides I had a chronic allergic rhinitis to dust mites and certain mold spores where sinus drainage would occasionally irritate my throat. I'd gargle with warm saltwater and take Cepacol lozenges to deaden any discomfort. Then if the throat weren't better in about a week, I'd see my doc. I knew that most common medical problems, like colds, tended to last about seven days and then disappeared.

However, this sore throat was worsening quickly. I tried not to breathe on Faust. I washed my hands frequently just in case. My temperature had risen to fever status with 104 degrees F. My ability to swallow was decreasing. Faust showed his concern by following me around the house everywhere I went and snuggling with me the moment I sat down. I covered my mouth to protect him. When he looked at me, scrutinizing my face, he'd cock his head to the right and let his whiskers droop. I could tell he wanted to help more than merely comforting me.

As I felt worse and wasn't paying as much attention to my daily chores, he also tried to alert me, by striking the side of his litter pan with his right paw, that I now wasn't policing it as frequently as I had in the past. Since he couldn't take care of it himself, he was reminding me that having to tiptoe around divots was unacceptable for a fastidious cat. As my condition worsened, I was becoming oblivious to lots of things, not just his requirement for litter sanitation. My face was getting redder. I was breathing harder. My heart was beating faster. At times I was feeling out of it which scared me ... and Faust. He seemed to know things weren't right and constantly watched me. He looked at me questioningly. There was little he could do besides looking antsy and concerned about what to do to make things better.

By the time I looked at my throat in the mirror, I was shocked. There were two necrotic-looking white bags of tissue, one on either side of my throat, that were approaching midline, ready to close off my breathing. Nearly delirious by now, I bundled up, locked up, left Faust mohwing loudly and piteously after me at the door to the basement, and headed for Newton-Wellesley Hospital's Emergency Room. On the road I was minimally successful staying awake, alert, and in my lane. I don't even remember arriving.

The ER physician looked askance as he examined me. He said, "You have a very bad case of bacterial tonsillitis. I'm surprised you still have your tonsils at your age."

Yeah, me too! I managed to gasp, "I had a tonsillectomy in 1948." I don't think he at first believed me. You know how physicians sometimes assume that patients don't have a clue about their bodies or what has been done to them or for them. Besides, how often is a bit of tonsil tissue left behind that actually re-grows itself into its full-blown organ. And this was obviously more than a bit of tissue that had survived on both sides. Besides, physicians are loath to criticize another physician for his or her deficient work. He gave me an antibiotic prescription. However, I was left with the curious impression that he blamed me for the re-growth of my tonsils. Maybe that was my delirium speaking. But I was too sick to give a damn about what he may have or may not have thought or what I may have imagined. I have no idea how I drove home. Faust nearly knocked me down leaping into my arms.

At that time old standby antibiotics had not as yet been eclipsed by mega-bugs and were still effective with most bacteria. Even following a two-hour wait in the doctor's office for a ten-day re-check and several more regimens of penicillin, it took weeks for me to recover. And after all that physical and psychological childhood trauma of tonsil removal, I was definitely not electing to have it done again. "Fool me once, shame on you. Fool me twice ..."

When I first developed the sore throat, I threw together a mask of sorts from an old dish towel to make sure I didn't share any potential microbes with Faust. Of course, the fabric really didn't have small enough pores to prevent transmission of much of anything bacterial or viral. But I felt too unwell go out to check pharmacies for actual masks. Faust seemed to think it was great fun to swipe at the ersatz mask as if I were wearing it for him to play with. When I was seated, he'd come up from behind and nibble on the knot where I'd tied the ends together, his whiskers tickling my neck. Oh, Faust, that was foolhardy. His lungs were already sufficiently impaired when I found him that it might not take much of any bacterial infection, even in his throat, to put him in harm's way.

The mask and my constant hand washing may have, in the end, kept him safe. While it is rare for cats to have bacterial tonsillitis, I was told it could have occurred. As I endeavored to recover, I continued to wear the mask. This made Faust very happy. He also continued to keep me warm and safe until I was on my feet … and religiously scooping his litter pan once again.

13

"O TANNENBAUM"

Christmas was approaching and I needed something outdoors, fun, and different for us to do. To celebrate my good health, finally, I thought we'd take a trip to Rindge, New Hampshire. There was a Christmas tree farm I'd heard about that allowed people to choose their own tree to cut down. Whether we actually cut down a tree or not, I wanted to check it out. It had already snowed in New Hampshire so when we arrived, pristine snow covered the ground. The air was crisp and stimulating. The area was like a scene out of a favorite fairy tale with rows and rows of trees of differing sizes softly draped in glistening snow.

Wearing my red Eastern Mountain down coat, I placed Faust in its snap-attached down hood which lay on my upper back. He was also dressed a red acrylic-wool-combination body sweater I had knitted for him to wear under his harness. Together we trudged the tree plantation to look for our ideal tree. Faust had his head on a swivel as we slowly walked up and down the straight columns of adolescent fir and spruce trees.

I found myself grinning from ear to ear as I critically assessed each tree. Something so simple seemed so intoxicating to me. We were out in the cold, clear air, in the woods, amid hundreds of living Christmas trees, making our way through newly-fallen snow. I almost felt seasonally inspired. Yet, as I grew up, I had learned to hate Christmas. There was no spontaneity, no real festive spirit. It was a stressful ritual devoid of any happiness. Even cloyingly-spunky Tiny Tim would have been depressed. The very sound of Christmas carols always made me cry, and not tears of happiness.

Everything at Christmas had always been regimented, right on down to how many presents each person had to receive. You couldn't give the *one* perfect gift that someone truly wanted. It had to be one gift appropriate to that person and then whatever to fill out the quota. I used to agonize if my count was off because I couldn't figure out what little nothing to add to make the correct number. I hated wasting money on anything inconsequential. What was I going to do? I had to do something, anything. That felt so wrong.

Furthermore, it was also the season's prescription for my father to struggle mightily with setting up the tree, shouting and cursing, and not allowing anyone to point out that it might be leaning one way or another. No help from the peanut gallery was required. Blood pressures ran high. One year he hammered angled two-by-fours to the tree trunk then hammered those to floor-level pieces which he likewise hammered into the wood floor planks in the living room of our rented house. Even the delightfully pungent smell of balsam couldn't make it better.

And, of course, money was tight, as it usually was throughout the year. My mother worked two jobs and I worked three part-time ones around continuing my college classes. My father worked sporadically. At least some Christmases were, relatively speaking, better than others. But one year we were down to our last fifty cents with no food in the house to eat. The big decision was what edibles to buy with the change. My mother voted for a loaf of bread which would leave a little left over for something to put on it, like peanut butter, jelly, or cheese, to make some meals for us for a few days. But her family-survival common sense lost the debate. My nicotine-addicted father decided instead to use it to buy a pack of cigarettes that his body was clamoring for. While decades later, I forgave him for most of what he had done psychologically to me, I could never forgive him for that.

As I tromped through the snow, I was seeking but didn't locate the sharp scent of balsam which I loved. It was disappointing to learn that living trees were not as fragrant as trees with damaged or cut trunks or branches. If you wanted a tree to release its volatile oils, you had to do something harsh to it. Well, maybe pinching a tip might do it. Balsams and silver pines had what I considered the best Christmas tree smell because they had more bornyl acetate ("heart of pine") providing a woody fragrance because of fewer terpenes which provided the more turpentine scent in pines.

So many of the trees tickled my fancy. But then I came to a five-foot Frazer fir that looked the way I had imagined the ideal tree should look. It had soft, wide, flat needles that were silver-tinged on the underside. There was good spacing between branches to accommodate lights, ornaments, and tinsel. The bottom circumference was compact with no oddly-placed branches or bare spots. And the smell was nice but not balsam. But balsam firs looked and felt to me less sturdy. Visual beauty versus aroma. Like Faust, I'm more olfactory-oriented.

Faust wanted to get down. He plopped into the snow beside the Frazer fir then began to explore it. Suddenly he disappeared, only to be unearthed climbing to the top as the branches sagged and swayed under his weight, with their snow falling in clumps to the ground. Up popped his head, covered in white crystals, flashing his vampire incisors. He was in kitty heaven.

I loved the tree too but I didn't want to cut it down. Moreover, decorating it was a problem. In Sudbury for his and my first Christmas together I had bought a live four-foot tree in its large growing pot. Prior to Faust's arrival in my home, instead of a tree, I had placed several boughs of aromatic balsam on the side table in the living room on which I put silver and blue balls. But for Faust I decorated his tree with strings of colored lights and old family ornaments, many delicate

Norwegian and German hand-blown glass, handed down from my mother's mother. I was pleased with the beautiful, old-fashioned results. But after I had gone to bed, Faust went alpine. Perhaps thinking of himself as the feline Sir Edmund Hillary, he attempted his ascent. In clambering from branch to branch, he had managed to de-decorate the tree, dropping and smashing the ancient glass balls all over the wood floor.

When I heard the loud tinkling of glass, I jumped out of bed. "Oh, Faust! Dammit!" I exclaimed as I surveyed the damage. He looked happily at me as he was rolling the one ornament that somehow had managed not to break upon landing. I retrieved the dust pan and whisk broom to start the clean-up then finished with the vacuum cleaner just in case of minute particles. That was my fault. So dumb of me!

What was I to do then? After I cleaned up the glass slivers, denuded the tree for Faust, I went a little off-the-wall. I wanted to have something, anything, resembling a Christmas tree for me too. Looking around the first floor, I settled on decorating the five-foot-tall Monstera deliciosa, also known as the Swiss cheese plant or the Mexican breadfruit, that grew in the corner near the rear window. It had large, glossy green leaves with slits and holes on long leaf stalks which made it look like a thick pillar of shiny green. I had been growing it for years and it moved with me wherever I went.

Then I quickly scoured my "X-mas" boxes for any unbreakable ornamentation which I knew still existed from a

Christmas when I was in the fifth grade when we to make all our own ornaments. I put those boxes aside in the closet for tomorrow morning when I'd decorate the Monstera. That *could* work. After gathering the ornament which Faust was batting and chasing, I put it on a high shelf. It was time to go to bed … again. After Faust made one more climb, he joined me in bed. He used that tree every Christmas until it was growing too large for its pot and I could no longer handle it. I gave it to a next-door neighbor.

As I gazed at the beautiful Fraser fir, I immediately thought how Faust would gleefully repeat his performance with another tree. After all, he had just shown me how excited he was to have the opportunity to scale this pseudo-Everest again. Faust with eyes wide open and his whiskers raised was playing hide and seek among the branches, noticeably scented from the tree's perfume. He'd made his choice. This was *his* tree.

Maybe I should just purchase another live tree for Faust to enjoy. After the holiday, I could likewise keep it until it too outgrew its pot. And I would continue to decorate the Monstera, as I had every year since. What the heck. I'd grown used to doing that. Of course, colored lights were a no-no because of the danger of the heat on the delicate leaves. However, papier mâché balls covered in red, blue, green, and gold glitter, folded German stars made of foil paper, construction paper chains, rows of strung golden beads, and tinsel were sufficient for what mattered. And, even better, it was all unreachable by Faust.

When I located the salesperson, I inquired if they had any live trees either balled or in pots. As I expected, he didn't but he directed me, with a twang, to a nursery "down the road apiece" where I could likely find another Frazer fir in a pot. Surprisingly, the nursery did have some. None was as beautiful as the one Faust and I had picked out at the tree farm but they were would do. As long as Faust liked it.

I put Faust on the cold ground next to the five potted trees to see his reaction. He walked past each, sizing it up, then demonstrated his approval by scaling a four-footer without benefit of a Sherpa. They also had loose boughs of fragrant balsam which I purchased. In the end it had worked out well, even with the tricky maneuvers required for lifting the tree into the back of the car and tying it down. It had been an invigorating outing. Faust had his own Christmas tree again and I had my boughs to enjoy. Their spirit-lifting smells filled the car. Maybe Gordon or Michael might like the fir for their yard in a couple of years.

14

ADIEU, ALIX

After my best and oldest friend Alix's death, Faust and I took a few more trips to Northfield, Massachusetts, for cross-country skiing. She and I tried to go there at least several times each winter. Northfield Mountain Cross-Country Ski Area was located at an entirely underground hydroelectric-pumped storage facility–plant and artificial reservoir (formerly Northeast Utilities). The ski area provided twenty-five miles of groomed trails for classical and free-style skiing on Northfield Mountain at an elevation of 1,006 feet. The detailed trail maps marked the Expert trails, Hill and Dale, North Mountain, and Tooleybush Turnpike, in black. They were steep and super-fast. While I was there to do cross-country, the Expert trails provided me some downhill thrills.

One day I nearly had a bad accident on Hill and Dale where it perpendicularly meets Rock Oak Ramble. As I approached the intersection, I had been accelerating. Because of skiers who suddenly appeared to cross in front of Hill and Dale, I had to stop fast. I used a snow plough maneuver to slow down: ski tips together, arms forward, knees bent, weight on downhill ski, pressing it uphill. That was working fine until my left ski caught an icy patch. I did a split like a Thanksgiving turkey wishbone being snapped apart without time to make a wish. Oh my god! On one ski I missed the skiers, but lost my balance. However, I had made sure I fell forward. Faust was bundled in my knapsack on my back. On the gentler downward slopes when I wasn't propelling myself forward, either striding or side-to-side skating, I let Faust ride on the front of my narrow skis on the trails. This was something he had enjoyed for a short time until snow blowback frosted his fur enough to make him shiver. Hill and Dale was the first and only time we'd had a mishap. The resulting groin pull I sustained convinced me that Faust and I had had enough for that day.

But it was more than that. Skiing without Alix had lost a lot of its charm. If Faust wanted to do more cross-country, there was a large piece of wooded public land near our house where we could do our shushing. Possibly in the backyard as well. Maybe I'd make him his own skis so he could either rely on his own locomotion or, when he tired, be pulled along. Now if he could only learn how to push the snow with ski poles.

One time after Alix's death, Faust and I took trip to Walden Pond, one of her, my, and his favorite haunts, and where we had scattered her ashes. He had been crazy about her and the feeling was mutual. At first Faust sat solemnly on the shore, staring out across the water, twitching his ears but mostly ignoring the flies and mosquitoes buzzing around his head.

Then he turned his head and began looking back at the path we'd followed to get there, making little sounds, like "cheech," in his throat.

Suddenly my mind harkened back to Cheech Marin, half of Cheech and Chong. Damn. Where was that coming from? That was so inappropriate for the circumstance. But maybe I was trying to distract myself because I felt like weeping. I don't know if Faust remembered this location and associated it with the melancholy celebration of the end of her life, but I had the impression that he really didn't want to be there any longer. He just sat there, not batting at the flies, putting a paw in the water, or doing a dance step in her memory, things he did there when the three of us would visit. The loss was still too keen. I didn't want to be there either. We left and never returned.

Faust still had the colorful scarf she had bequeathed to him. Well, it was the one she had impishly had placed in her casket for him to find at the viewing. He, with the help of the funeral home's misinformed and prissy personnel, created the most riotously memorable viewing in their history. I have no doubt that Alix had laughingly anticipated it by the directions she had left. That was so "Alix." She would always be alive in my heart. But I really wanted her here at my side instead.

15

DR. DEMENTO

The American Psychological Association had chosen my research on ubiquitous sex-role stereotypes that I had done for one of my master's degrees to be presented at their huge convention in D.C. It looked at how people responded to newspaper articles about female candidates for office when they were described neutrally or by the sexist terms that were commonly used in the media for women at that time. When the sexist terms were used, the candidate was significantly devalued, seen as less leaderlike, strong, and capable than when described in neutral terms. No surprise there. But maybe it would help point out the need for non-sexist language in newspapers.

To fly or drive? Of course, flying was preferable but I decided to drive down instead. Faust had flown to and from Florida to see my mother without any difficulty with the airline. That is, if you ignored the cat hater who constantly complained to the flight attendant that Faust shouldn't exist, much less fly *inside* the plane. Her dog with its red-painted toe nails and bows that had had to be sedated for the entire trip was okay to be in the passenger compartment but my quiet, well-behaved, non-sedated cat wasn't.

However, this other airline whose flight schedule for D.C. aligned with mine wasn't as eager to allow him in the passenger compartment. I pushed and they pushed back. That was a large problem because there was *no* way he was going to travel in the cargo hold, at risk of freezing, losing oxygen, being squashed by some shifting or falling pieces of "luggage," or being dumped unseen in a luggage shuttle or holding room. However, four hundred and thirty-nine miles was a dauntingly long way to drive, taking about eight hours. Words cannot express my level of "pure glee" at my anticipation of it. Oh, well. We'd try to make it an excursion.

Before we started in the car, I gathered together about fifteen audio cassettes of Dr. Demento radio programs I had taped to ease the boredom of driving. The "Dr." was an American radio broadcaster and record collector who specialized in novelty songs, comedy, and strange or unusual recordings dating from the early days of shellac and vinyl phonograph records to the present. He played such notable pieces from personalities from an earlier time as Slacker Radio's Stan Freberg's "Bang Gunnleigh U.S. Marshall Field" and "St. George and the Dragonet," "Weird Al" Yankovic's "Dare to be Stupid" and "Christmas at Ground Zero," and Tom Lehrer singing "Vatican Rag" or "Poisoning Pigeons in the Park." One of my favorites was Randy Rivera singing, "Sally

Ann," which was an alternative version of "Sing Me a Country Western Song." It was the droll tale of how a psychopath deals with romantic rivals. What a hoot!

When I looked through the cassettes to choose the entertainment, I discovered that a number of them were missing from their slots. That included the BBC Radio 4's original 1978 production of Douglas Adams' *The Hitchhiker's Guide to the Galaxy.* They had been stored in small open trays beside the VHS tapes near the television in the dining room. J.P. was the only one who had been in there with the tapes. That also brought to mind how after we had returned from D.C. and he had to use the bathroom that a sterling silver seal pin with an 18-karat gold ball on a spring above its nose that my mother had given me had disappeared from my dresser. At the time I thought that, perhaps, it was only misplaced. But I never found it. After the cassettes also had disappeared, I changed my mind. It reminded me that in his screenplay of *House of Games* David Mamet had his character "Mike" refer to "Dr. Margaret Ford," his con game victim who stole his penknife, as a "booster." That was too kind a term for J.P.

By the time of my APA presentation I had worked the kinks out of my eight-hour cramped legs. The presentation went well. The slide projector functioned properly. I had a large group of listeners who seemed interested and asked questions. For it I wore a nicely tailored cranberry-colored light-weight wool suit. Whenever I wore it, I felt particularly competent. I still associate that outfit with success. Because

Faust had had to stay in my hotel room while I gave my talk, I had promised him I'd take him out afterward. I changed into cotton slacks and a loose blouse and we left.

Wearing his harness and leash and stuffed in his knapsack on my shoulders, he accompanied me to the Smithsonian's National Zoo where a baby panda had just been born. I crouched, twisted, kneeled to see into their den but mom and baby smartly remained hidden, elusive. We hung around for thirty minutes, as I continued to contort my body to somehow, hopefully, penetrate the darkness, to catch even a glimpse of the mama munching on some bamboo. But no such luck. Faust, who liked to be moving around, unless he was watching something stimulating, acted bored. He was wriggling in his knapsack, looking this way than that. This kind of delayed gratification was not his thing.

I was surprised to learn that the panda baby, though born in the U.S., was not a birthright "citizen." At the age of three or four, when it reached sexual maturity, it would likely go back home to China for breeding purposes. You could call it a sort of Panda Lend-Lease. Not altogether different from the policy signed into law in 1941 to defeat Germany, which ended when the war with Japan ended. The original Lend-Lease, however, was about aid and free distribution of food, oil, materiel, warships, warplanes, and weaponry, instead of pandas. Pandas are a big moneyed deal for China.

Now scouring the zoo for interesting animals, especially

ones that would grab Faust's attention, I saw the tail of a tiger returning to its cage in behind the concrete wall. Faust's head, leaning over my shoulder, followed it. A cheetah was lying on an artificial branch about ten feet up, snoozing, only occasionally swishing its tail. Faust craned his neck to see if the cheetah were awake or asleep. Western low-land gorillas were sitting around on the grass, grooming, and the young ones were chasing and wrestling. Faust looked at them, cocked his head to the right. I could see him stare at me in my peripheral vision. He looked confused. Was he wondering if his servant and these furry critters were related? Was he assigning value to the differences? I'm not sure how I would have come out in that comparison, except that I was the one who offered him food and back rubs and they didn't. That was a point for me.

It was a humid ninety degrees so most of the animals were taking a siesta in whatever shade they could find. That was a good idea. We found an ornate wrought iron and wood bench along the path under some tree, one of the 180 species of trees there. For a few minutes we people-watched and considered out next move.

Any time I'm around wild animals in captivity I feel conflicted. On the one hand, I'm glad to be able to see them, more-or-less up close and personal, but not in their true natural environments. Few zoos had really great quarters for them or lots of natural space in which to move about comfortably. On the other, I wanted them to roam free, living their lives as Nature intended … as predators or prey animals … but—and this was the rub—*protected* from trophy hunters and poachers. In the zoos they were safe but at what cost. Safety over freedom. I knew which one I'd pick for me personally ... and for them.

That reminded me of Koko, the zoo-born, female low-land gorilla. Francine "Penny" Patterson was her caretaker at the San Francisco Zoo when the baby had a life-threatening illness. Patterson then became her instructor and caregiver for her doctoral research at Stanford University on inter-species communication, using a modified version of American Sign Language. It was wonderful to follow Koko's adventures in learning after she moved to a preserve in Woodside, California.

While some researchers in great-ape language disputed Koko's accomplishments, Koko demonstrated she was able to understand some two thousand words of spoken English. She communicated by sign but without syntax and grammar, like a young child. Patterson's work quickly brought gorillas to the public's awareness and they loved everything Koko did, especially when she adopted a kitten she gently cared for. Koko became popular because of her similar emotional and cognitive capacities.

She lived a relatively-speaking "good" life, which included opportunities to mate with male gorilla companions, Michael and Ndume, she but didn't. Maybe that was because they felt like siblings. Still, she continued to show that she wanted a real gorilla baby. Part of me felt bad that she grew up psychologically part-gorilla and part-human and that she couldn't ever experience living in the wild.

Finally, after checking out the reptile enclosure, which Faust did not appear to like, especially the snakes, I walked back to the hotel. Along the way I bought three apples and four packs of peanut butter crackers from a neighborhood grocery for our trip home. I already had a bag of crunchies for Faust stashed in the car. My body would punish me for it. While our short stay at the conference and zoo was fun, after a good night's sleep, it would be another eight straight hours—480 minutes—of leg-spasmed-driving and listening to Dr. Demento tapes. That was an ordeal I was more than willing to forego in the future. Next time I'd fly, hiding Faust in under-seat stowed, vented carry-on luggage, if necessary.

16

CALIFORNIA DREAMIN'

I'd promised Faust well before we moved to Wellesley that we'd finally take a trip to California sometime in the near future. I'd been promising this for a long time. Every so often Faust would glance at me with that "you know what you promised and I'm being so patient waiting for it" look in his eye. I'd know immediately what he was referring to and feel guilty. Cats are especially good at infusing you with guilt but Faust was a past master at it. So after nearly two years in Wellesley, I decided we should finally take our extended trip. I had planned for us to be gone for three weeks to spend our time in Death Valley. That was overly optimistic.

Initially I thought we would drive but discovered from AAA it would take forty-three hours to cover 2,853 miles. If we could manage ten hours a day every day, that would be over four days and we'd be exhausted when we arrived. That wouldn't include any sightseeing or letting Faust and me stretch our cramping legs every several hours. Ten hours of pedal to the metal, stopping only to use a restroom and grabbing food and drink on the fly, did not appeal to me. From past experience, our road trip to D.C., for example, I knew energetic Faust would become bored and frustrated after several hours and begin bouncing off the walls. He was already psyched to tackle the wildlife in the hottest place in the world, just not ride in the car. And I knew that when we finally arrived, after unpacking the car and setting up Faust, I would just throw myself on a motel bed and sleep for twenty hours straight.

If I thought that was bad, we'd be doing that twice, going and coming. That meant we'd spend ten days out of twenty-one just non-stop traveling, with only eleven to casually explore everything on our list of attractions and anything else that might pop up. And that, of course, would also involve driving. Therefore, it made a lot more sense to fly to Las Vegas which would take only five hours and then rent a car to ferry us to Death Valley. Death Valley was only another one hundred twenty-three miles which would take us about two hours to drive. We could get a motel room near McCarren Airport, where we'd land, and start fresh in the morning.

That settled, I made all the arrangements for the trip. Then I stopped the mail, left the electricity on to run the timer for the house lights, but turned off the water to the house. I remembered all too well my mother's swampy surprise when she returned from a two-day trip. Her kitchen was flooded with four inches of water and her living room carpet was submerged. If you weren't splashing, you were squishing.

Fortunately, there were no alligators or poisonous snakes in the ankle-deep water. A hose coupling under the kitchen sink had failed.

The car was packed with our clothing, a small folded tent and sleeping bag. We were ready to decamp first thing in the morning of the day after tomorrow. Then I slapped my forehead! Dummy! What about the car? I couldn't leave it in long-term parking for three weeks. It would cost a fortune and it probably would no longer have wheels when we returned. It probably wouldn't have been stolen in toto because it wasn't chop shop material.

There was the train that stopped in Wellesley which went all the way into South Station where I could pick up a bus to Logan Airport. It would take us over an hour total and cost about $20. However, since I didn't want to walk to the train station loaded down like a pack mule, juggling Faust and luggage, I'd have to call a cab. That could work, just barely.

After I repacked, I made an arrangement for a cab to pick us up at an unholy hour so we could catch the 6:34 a.m. train for a 10:50 a.m. flight. It all seemed to be cutting it a little close but 6:34 a.m. was the earliest departure time. Damn! If only I could drive into Boston, it would take us about twenty-four minutes, a few bucks in tolls, and provide lots of comfortable latitude. Yeah, if only I had an invisibility cloak for the car at the airport or could find a sky hook. I didn't know anyone in Boston who would have anything as rare as an "extra" parking space which could be available to me.

That night I thought about having been in Southern California much earlier on, well before Faust. I had worked at Fairview State Hospital (later called Fairview Developmental Center) in Costa Mesa, with behaviorist Dr. Thomas Ball. I worked with developmentally disabled individuals, doing behavioral therapy research with moderately-affected individuals. I worked to determine how to intermittently reward individuals to get them out of their chairs to walk around to get exercise. By the time I finished that internship, I had one individual walking around the entire building in one session. I suspect she may have been unable to appreciate what she had accomplished because of her condition, but I appreciated it. Unfortunately, as was to be expected, once I stopped with her, she fell back into her routine of sitting all the time. I hoped someone else would take up the exercise regimen with her but with the shortage of techs, I suspected it wasn't likely to happen.

While there I also participated in two projects. One was with post-near-drowning victims. The project explored the use of neurological tests of smell on those who had nearly drowned to determine the degree of brain damage in comatose survivors and the likelihood of their incipient deaths. The subjects of these tests responded on EEG to a decreasing sensory response to sound and touch. When they no longer reacted to those specific stimulations, their brains still responded to smell. However, as they approached death, they appeared to show brain activity only to the strongest of smells. And when death was imminent, they no longer responded to even that.

While it is often thought that hearing is the last sense to go before death, it appeared that the oxygen-deprived brain of post-near drowning victims may have altered that. I never saw their final conclusions because I had left to go back to Massachusetts, to be "coddled and pampered" by Boston University's doctoral program as my associate on the project referred to it.

My associate was a tall, blond-haired, cowboy-boot-wearing Nazi enthusiast who had Third Reich memorabilia on the walls of his office and played Audiophile vinyl recordings of Hitler's speeches. The most prominent feature of his personality was his anger. He was a constantly irate individual who stated he believed that every minority, including me as a female, was getting into Ph.D. programs because of Affirmative Action. According to him, my good grades, being smart, my other degrees, and relevant activities had nothing to do with my being accepted. Instead, he said, "It was favoritism of the worst kind ... reverse discrimination ... and I'm being royally shafted as a result. It's so unfair!"

He repeatedly and vituperatively stated, "Gender and skin color matter more than my being a white male." He couldn't understand why his white male cultural entitlement didn't supersede everything else. It was obvious to him, as he spouted his discontent to me between chain-smoked cigarettes, "There was no way you could possibly have achieved what you have on your own merit. Specifically, you would never have been accepted into Boston University's psychology doctoral program if it had not been for the undeserved, gender-bias-prescribed help you received!"

Being around him alone made me uncomfortable, especially in his office surrounded by symbols of hate. It had occurred to me that his attitude and sense of blind outrage about perceived discrimination against him particularly, but against white males generally, made him potentially violent and, maybe, even dangerous. Consequently, when he ranted about his favorite topic, I didn't argue with him about it. When being an unintentional captive audience, I only listened with "rapt attention," looking at him thoughtfully as if I were carefully weighing his "interesting" ideas. As I recalled him, I couldn't help wondering what he did when he wasn't listening to Hitler and grousing about the vanishing power and right of domination "correctly" accorded to white males.

The other project on which I worked was on assertiveness training with mildly and moderately developmentally-disabled individuals. It was a new program designed to allow them greater social freedom, access to and interaction with the community at large. We would engage them in simulated situations and suggest how to ask questions for information, respond to others' questions, and how to ask for what they wanted. They also had to learn how to handle money and identifying themselves.

The big problem was to get them to focus and keep them focused while they heard the phrases to use in each situation and what they meant. Then it was a matter of repetition and association in role playing and getting them to generalize specifics. The goal was to allow them to use public transportation and arrive where they wanted. To confidently go to a restaurant or store to buy what they wanted. To speak with a police officer when they needed help. To move about more comfortably in their neighborhood and community.

These individuals were very endearing because of their innocence, trustfulness, and naiveté, seeing the world as only good and friendly. Because of their lack of awareness of the many facets of people as individuals and in groups, the program was particularly important. After having worked with assertiveness training for some time myself, I was sure this project was on the right track in how it provided a social benefit to a set of developmentally-disabled people who really needed this assistance to live more independently. I wanted it to succeed and be a model for many other programs in California and beyond. Unfortunately, once again, I left before an assessment of the project was done.

17

FLYING IN THE JOHN

At Logan with a few minutes to spare I got Faust's small, flat, gray airline kitty carrier and squeezed him into it, not without his complaint. I was struggling with my overnight bag, which contained several changes of clothing, toiletries, Faust's disposable litter pan and a small bag of clay litter, and my three-foot canvas tote which contained the folded-up tent, compacted sleeping bag, empty camping stove, my hiking boots, and utensils. I had granola bars, kitty treats, and a hardback book in my messenger bag. I planned on purchasing fuel for the stove, packages of freeze-dried food, and Gatorade in Death Valley. I stowed the canvas tote in the overhead and kept the overnight at my feet, under the seat in front of me. Faust's carrier was on my lap. He'd be released from his duck press prison as soon as the plane was in the air. If no one took the seat next to me, it would have been all his if he wanted it. Since no one did, he intermittently took advantage of it.

He sat comfortably on my lap as I read Robin Cook's latest formulaic thriller until I had to use the restroom. With Faust back in his airline carrier, I hauled him and his folded litter pan and bag of litter down the aisle to the first unoccupied john. I hadn't recalled how little space was available in the cubicle. Oops! Big problem. Where would I place his carrier? With one hand I held it at a forty-five-degree angle in the half-size sink with the other hand I attempted to unzip my slacks. Progress was slow as my bladder called louder for relief.

As my trousers dropped toward the floor, I involuntarily reached for them, to keep them from hitting it as well. But as I did, Faust's carrier followed suit. It snapped open as it hit the floor. Faust gingerly extricated himself, frightened and slightly battered. With barely enough room to jump into the sink, he leapt and slipped, hitting the door. All this time I was trying to squat over the bowl, silently urging my urinary bladder sphincter to relax and release. Faust frantically pawed at the door like a trapped bobcat. "No, Faust, don't do that. I'll get you out of here as soon as possible. Pleeeeze, Faust!"

As I was bending over to remove Faust from the door, my bladder finally let loose. Urine hit the toilet rim and sprayed all over the bathroom. In my juggling act I'd become misaligned with the bowl. There was quite a mess to clean up when I was finished. Faust looked at me as if begging me to rescue him. When I didn't respond right away, he tried to climb on to my non-existent lap. "No, not now, Faust." Then he tried to sit on my lowered trousers, between my legs. "No!" I attempted to remove him. I had to re-dress myself but I couldn't pull my slacks up with him there. He looked up at me with lowered ears as if I were disowning him.

Minutes passed. I managed to put myself together. With a handful of paper towels, I attempted to dry everything in sight, especially Faust's open carrier which was wedged between the toilet and sink support. Since he hadn't tried to urinate anyplace in the restroom, I made the assumption he didn't have to go. I hoped I was correct. I disentangled the carrier, re-squeezed Faust into it and washed my hands one at a time as I had to use the other hand to hold his carrier on the sink.

When we eventually slipped out through the door, there were several other anxious-looking people waiting. I whispered, "Sorry," and sheepishly returned to my seat. At least Faust hadn't been showered during my baptism by urine, though I have no idea how he managed it without aerial rigging. Sometimes you have to be grateful for whatever little benefit you can summon.

18

RUDE AWAKENING

The Avis car we rented was a standard Ford Pinto, the seat belt of which cut across my throat. The seat's two positions placed me either too close to the dashboard where my knees hit the steering wheel or too far from the accelerator, clutch, and brake. This was definitely not going to work. I trudged back to the rental desk and asked for another vehicle. This time I got a Honda Accord hatchback which fitted me fine. This car also provided a Las Vegas map.

There were several motels in the airport area most of which had a vacancy. I closed my eyes and picked one. We arrived late and lugged our gear up one flight and along several long, sterile, monochromatic hallways to our room. Since I didn't want to leave anything in the rental car that might attract thieves, I made an extra trip to make sure everything was cleaned out or hidden. It was still early enough to find food so we checked the Yellow Pages of the Las Vegas phone book. While the motel had a restaurant, I tended to avoid motel restaurant food. For some reason they seemed to over-steam their canned vegetables, leaving them even more mushy or leave the prepared plate soaking up drying radiation under the infrared heating lamps.

As a vegetarian, I wasn't interested in fast-food joints. Faust, however, offered to sacrifice himself and have whatever McDonald's or Wendy's offered, as long as it had some vague similarity to meat, with the right amount of tasty grease and salt. Lucky him, he wasn't concerned about fats and cholesterol in his diet as some of us were.

There was a small adobe restaurant near the motel which offered Mexican food. How authentically "Mexican" it was, I didn't know but could guess. The menu featured a large taco bowl so I ordered it with chicken on the side, for Faust. All the mixed greens and tomatoes looked great with the avocado, black beans, sour cream, and red and green salsa. I slipped Faust out of his knapsack onto to a chair I pulled next to me and placed his sandwich plate of chicken on it. We enjoyed our meals. Ruminating upon fats and cholesterol, I had to skip the deep-fried taco shell as much as I really wanted to pig out on it.

After we returned to our light green room, I plopped into a floral over-stuffed chair and fiddled with the TV remote. Instead of curling around my shoulders, Faust jumped onto the bed and began sniffing. I figured some previous occupant had had a dog or cat in room on the bed. Enjoy yourself, Faust, I thought as I scanned the local channels, the motel amenities, and ads for soft porn movies. Big whoop-dee-doo. Faust was now vigorously scratching the forest green bedspread. I leaned over to brush him away, "Don't! You'll tear the fabric!" but I missed. I hoped he'd calm down when I actually got into bed. The national channels were grainier and offering either Lawrence Welk and his bubble machine or the weather. Thank you so much. I'll pass. I was ready for sleep anyway.

As I changed into my man's medium tee-shirt as my pajamas, Faust was trying mightily to slither under the bedspread. "Faust, for heaven's sake, just relax. We'll be in bed shortly." I pulled the bedspread back to ease his access and went to the bathroom to wash my face and brush my teeth. In the bathroom mirror, I could see him now digging, trying to get under the blanket. As I rinsed my mouth, I wondered what his problem was. I expected—sincerely hoped—he wouldn't be so wired or obsessed while I tried to sleep.

"Okay, *now* it's bedtime," I said to him. My eyelids were already at half-mast. As I pulled back the blanket and sheet, I mentally shrieked. "Oh my god! Goddamn son of a bitch!" In the middle of the queen-size bed was a urine-soaked bath towel! It looked as if someone had invited a musk ox into bed … and oops! It was still wet.

Faust went crazy, digging at the edges of the towel while I kneeled down on the beige carpeting to reach under the bed. How bad was it? The mattress was wet all the way through. Someone had given changing the bed linen short shrift. I could picture the maid rushing about, seeing the bed was already made, saying, "Good. That's off my list," and going on to some other task.

I took deep breaths. But when I shouted at Faust to stop, my voice was rising. I sat back down on the floral chair and unsuccessfully pretended to meditate. "Shit! Shit! Shit! Faust get away from there." I leapt for the bed, shoved him under my arm, and stowed him in the bathroom.

Standing by the puddle of liquid nitrogenous waste which seemed to stare up at me, smugly saying, "Lots of luck," I called the front desk for the manager. Faust had begun to rapidly scratch the bathroom door, commanding me to let him out of there ... pronto. Just then I heard a voice on the line.

"What can I do for you?" the male asked.

"We have a serious problem. There is a urine-soaked bath towel in the middle of the bed in Room 236. I want another room."

"There are no other rooms available."

"Then I want another mattress. This one is soaked clear through."

"I can have someone come flip the mattress and make the bed."

"I don't think you understand. The urine has soaked through to the other side. The mattress is wet. It's not acceptable."

"Well, I can provide you with a rollaway bed."

"I didn't pay for a bare-bones, uncomfortable, sleep-defying rollaway. I paid for a comfortable queen-size bed."

"I don't know what else you expect me to do."

"I expect you to provide what I paid for." There was air on the line. "Okay," I continued, "if that's not going to happen, I'm checking out right now. As a result, I expect *not* to be billed for this room. I'll be down momentarily to hand back the room key and get my charge slips."

"But once you checked in, you made the room unavailable to anyone else."

"No, your maid who didn't change the bed or alert you to the problem made the room unavailable to me and anyone else."

"Well, I have to charge you something."

"No, this is not debatable."

"So *what* are you going to do about it?"

I couldn't believe this bozo was challenging me over *their* error. One unhappy customer could be very bad for business, especially when the complaint had to do with something as disgusting as a urine-soaked bath towel in the bed. He ought to know that bad word of mouth always travels faster than good.

"Since you asked," I said calmly, "I think it would be

appropriate to let the media know what a careless establishment you have. A photo of the problem would be a stunning graphic accompaniment."

"Fine!" he said angrily and hung up.

When I let Faust out of the bathroom to put him in his carrier, he lunged for the bed and re-attacked the wet towel with his back feet. Then suddenly he seemed ready to squat to cover it with his own scent. "Faust!" I rebuked him as I quickly leaned over the side of the bed to grab him, "Don't you dare piss on that." He didn't but looked both hurt and mystified. I'd made an assumption I hadn't validated. Maybe he would have, maybe not, but most likely he would have. At this moment it didn't matter. I unceremoniously shoved him into his carrier.

Re-dressed, I hauled Faust and all our gear back down to the car, double-checked the room, and dropped the key at the front desk *only after retrieving all copies* of my charge slip. We drove around the neighborhood, found another motel which had a room available and where they would let me check the bed *before* signing in. "O frabjous joy!" IT WAS DRY! And it wasn't a rollaway. As soon as I once again lugged everything back to the room, Faust and I hit the sack. Ahhhh. Sleep was divine!

"What happens in Las Vegas stays in Las Vegas"? Boy, I hoped so!

19

DEATH VALLLEY, HERE WE COME

Feeling refreshed and with a complimentary breakfast staving off hunger, we took off around 8:30 a.m. traveling I-95 to Rt. 73 for our drive to Death Valley Junction. I had a long list of where I wanted us to go in Death Valley, assuming all the roads, which were mostly gravel, were passable. The list was really way too long so I'd have to decide what to delete. I wanted it all planned out by the most efficient route. Our first stop after Death Valley Junction was the Amargosa Opera House on Rt. 90.

When we arrived in the large, gravel parking lot, I spotted the building labelled "opera house." It was singularly unimpressive-looking. A two-story-appearing, boxy, white-washed Spanish Colonial Revival adobe building, it resembled a 1930s YMCA. Stretching off to its left was a long, one-level, twenty-three-room hotel with a dining room. I hadn't read much about the opera house but had been told by traveling friends, "You absolutely have to see it." Were they really talking about *this*?

According to its history, in 1967 ballerina Marta Becket rented what had been the recreation hall for the Pacific Coast Borax Company town in order to stage mime and dance performances. After making repairs, she went ballistically artistic. She created sets, painted murals on the adobe walls, and renamed the building after its original mining town, Amargosa. In 1970 *National Geographic* highlighted her accomplishment, an issue I had missed. *Life* magazine had done a profile on her as well, something I likewise had missed. I didn't specifically check this at the Wellesley Library. Consequently, I had no idea what to expect.

When she finished in 1974, she established this as a non-profit foundation. Then she replaced the garden-chair seating with one hundred and twenty theater seats from a theater in Boulder City, Nevada, making it even grander. People from all over the world had visited and enjoyed performances from such notables as Red Skelton and Ray Bradbury as well as Marta Becket. It was open all-year round. As interesting as that was to read, it just didn't prepare me for the interior of the opera house.

After I parked, I tucked Faust into his knapsack and we headed in. Wow! What a wonderful surprise! The two-tier-high walls were covered with murals of seated Spanish noble men and women and nuns in a painted balcony which curved from the entry wall onto each side. The common folks were pictured seated on the main floor below the balcony. Everyone was in rapt attention to whatever performances were being held there. On the lower side walls moving toward the stage area were tableaus of entertaining circus acts, like jugglers and acrobats. The ceiling was painted medium-light blue with birds in flight, cherubs holding banners, and folds in the corners as if the ceiling cover were fabric. In the center was a huge antiqued gold medallion with seated Greek female musicians, each playing a different instrument, circling the perimeter. A single dove in flight entering the medallion was its grace note.

Faust seemed fascinated by the colors and shapes, staring and reaching out to touch the figures in the murals. The circus performers were of particular interest. We took our time examining all Becket's paintings: the caricatures and brush strokes. There was so much detail that was not caught in a quick glance. She had done an amazing job. I wondered if she had used a scaffold and platform, as Michelangelo had done for the Sistine Chapel, in order to do this ceiling. I couldn't imagine trying to paint while on my back.

After almost a half-hour in the opera house, we moseyed down past the motel rooms, checking them out through their front windows, and into the dining room. While we were having a bite of lunch, we could hopefully determine our next series of sights to visit. As was becoming very obvious—something I hadn't fully recognized from looking at larger maps—the distances between sites in Death Valley were much greater than I had assumed. For example, Scotty's Castle was forty-five miles from Stove Pipe Wells, where I was planning to stay when we weren't camping, and then another twenty-nine miles from there to the Racetrack Playa where boulders "mysteriously" moved across the surface. Ubehebe Crater was even farther north. To catch the Devil's Golf Course we had to travel well south of Stove Pipe Wells.

At least it appeared that most of the roads were accessible without a four-wheel-drive vehicle. Well, I guessed, that was as long as it hadn't rained. Then things were probably up for grabs. The result was going to be heavily time-consuming, s-l-o-w driving.

From the opera house we turned south to Furnace Creek and the visitor's center, passed Zabriskie Point, and headed to the Stove Pipe Wells Village, our immediate destination. It was situated near the Mesquite Flat Sand Dunes and Mosaic Canyon, which, hopefully would be easy to see on our way to other more demanding sites.

On a whim, I decided to inspect Mesquite Flat Sand Dunes immediately before we checked in. Taking Sand Dunes Road from Rt. 190, we followed the unpaved road to a field of beige-gold sand which seemed to go on forever before hitting the mountains. A STOP sign greeted us. Through symbols it stated: No dogs, no smoking, no camping. We could handle that. The dunes weren't all that high, with the highest being about one hundred feet in elevation, but there were some marked differences among them. The booklet I had stated that there were three types of dune configurations: crescent, linear, and star-shaped. Even though it would have been easier to see from the air, I could make out some dunes that had wave-like sand; some had straight parallel lines; some peaked. While some of the sand felt hard enough to walk on without sinking in, other areas were softer. Was the softer sand hard enough for a seven-pound cat to traverse on the surface? I'd wanted to change from my Nike running shoes into my hiking boots for trekking across it.

While I mulled this over, Faust was scanning the dunes. His focus seemed to land on the small leguminous mesquite trees growing everywhere, dispersed near and far, forming large, stable hummocks. Mesquite was considered invasive in Southern California. It could grow as a small shrub in shallow soil or up to fifty feet in better soil with adequate moisture. The trees at Sand Dunes had multiple trunks and multiple branches. Yellow flower spikes were beginning to form amid the delicate, light green bipinnate leaves. At some point they'd form long bean pods, which when dried, could be ground into flour. When Faust and I hiked the dunes, we'd have to examine them carefully, being aware that some of the forty species of mesquite had thorns.

Where mesquite had died, their shallow roots having been pulled up by winds, there were twisted skeletal trunks and branches. Some of the smaller pieces reminded me of driftwood. As Faust began pulling on his leash in that direction, I suspected Faust was considering marching to them ... now. Wildlife was undoubtedly living there among the clustered trees, some of which might find a cat very appealing.

Maybe lip smacking good. Even if Faust was ready to check them out, I wasn't. Not just yet.

In our rustic room in the rough-hewn-looking, dark khaki-stained, vertical-sided, one-story motel we unpacked, made a pit stop, then headed across the way from the Stove Pipe Wells Campground to three-mile-long Mosaic Canyon. It was at an elevation of 1,200 feet. Once parked, we began hiking. Within the first quarter of a mile, the rocky wash which leads into the canyon narrows and you're surrounded by smooth marble walls. The layered boulder surfaces had been scoured and polished by grit-laden flash floods.

Faust wanted to get out of his knapsack to wander around. I placed him at my feet and he began to explore the few feet of the flatter canyon floor which accepted the coefficient of friction of his pads until the marble sides began to rise upward. He slowly started sliding back. Then he initiated scrambling movements which speeded up his downward movement. His look was one of confusion and frustration. He'd tackled trees, rocks, and all kinds of natural surfaces with success. So what was going on now? Even with my running shoes I was finding some surfaces slippery and my balance less than perfect. Would my stiffer hiking boots be any better? Since the canyon was so close to the motel, we could try it at another time.

We turned around and drove south for twenty-five miles for Artists' Palette Drive. This was a one-way loop where we could enjoy the eye-catching chemical spectrum that flowed across the slopes. Large quasi-horizontal bands of red, pink, yellow, cocoa, and pistachio green stains followed the contours of the mountains. Chemical weathering and hydrothermal alteration had created a chemical reaction which oxidized different minerals, such as iron, tuff-derived mica, and manganese. It all looked like a vanilla ice cream parfait done with different layers of light-colored syrups.

To round out the afternoon, Faust and I drove south on 190 to Badwater Road in search of the Devil's Golf Course. This was a two-hundred-square-mile salt pan, almost three hundred feet *below* sea level in the Mojave Desert, within the eastern part of Death Valley. I had seen pictures of these strangely-craggy boulders in Badwater Basin. They ranged for as far as the eye could see. But at a distance, they gave me no idea about their size or exceedingly dangerous appearance. It was said that it had gotten its name because some wag had declared "only the devil could play golf on it."

After I ventured closer to the boulders, I was astounded. Some were huge. The spikiness of these dirty-gray, sand-and-dirt-included halite salt crystal boulders looked as if they were sharp enough to pierce the soles of your shoes. Some areas looked smoother as if trampled by tourists. I was sure the boulders with spires could do untold bad and bloody things to any part of your body that collided with them.

I had told Faust he could explore too, but had second thoughts about it when I saw X-ACTO knife blade-like projections everywhere. Instead, I removed him from his knapsack at the very edge of the golf course, put him on a tight leash, and only let him sniff them. It was abundantly clear his pawing at them was dangerous. He strained, trying to get the proper leverage to force me to give him some slack. I don't think he quite had a handle on the physics of his moves. I picked him up and tip-toed us some distance to a flatter, smoother place amid the boulders where we could stand. Here I could let him feel he was able to check things out … a little. That is, until he decided to—ack!—try to mount one of the spiny boulders. No! No! No!

Where he had started to place his weight was a thin, nearly horizonal thick crystal cluster which broke off before it could do any damage to his pads. He let out a small mohw as the broken crystal shard brushed his pads. He backed off carefully, apparently convinced that standing on this particular boulder wouldn't work. However, that incident didn't stop his curiosity. After all, it could have been a fluke. He was poised to try again.

I was bending over examining the makeup of a boulder when I caught a glimpse of him. Oh, no! He was just about to step directly on a narrow vertical crystal. I grabbed him, lifted him up, and stuffed him back into his knapsack. Only his head was exposed as I tightened the opening around him.

Initially he looked more surprised than angry. I could hear him thinking, "Humans are such anxious creatures." This place wasn't safe for a curiosity-driven feline. I turned to escape. If my foot placement and balance hadn't been of primary concern, I would have gently carried Faust back out of this pedal labyrinth in my arms. But I needed my arms available to flap, if necessary, in order to keep my equilibrium. It took five long minutes until I could make my way back safely to non-crystallized terra firma.

As soon as I touched smoother ground, Faust demonstrated how unhappy he was. Mohwing loudly, he wriggled his body. His hind feet scratched my back as he attempted to gain purchase in the fabric and squeeze from his carrier. He shoved his right paw past his head, waving it around like a flag until he could secure his claws in my shoulder blade in an endeavor to pull himself out.

I squeaked in pain, "Ooh! Damn. Thank you so much, Faust. I think it's time to call it a day. Tomorrow we can see Scotty's Castle, the Racetrack Playa, and maybe Ubehebe Crater. That work for you?" When he settled down, I took that as agreement.

That evening after a meal from what we had bought at the Stovepipe Wells General Store across the way, we lay outside a short distance away from the building on the sleeping bag I'd brought. I looked up at the incredible vast blanket of white points of light against the impenetrable blackness. With so little ambient illumination from the ground to interfere with visualizing the stars, I was absolutely overwhelmed by the surrounding immensity and beauty of it all, the awesome reaches of infinity.

It reminded me of lines of John Keats' "Ode on a Grecian Urn," "Beauty is truth, truth beauty—that is all ye know on earth, and all ye need to know." Except that I didn't agree with "that was all ye need to know." Exploring the cosmos, looking for shadows of knowledge, must be so obsessively exciting. I couldn't wait for the next astronomical discovery.

I immediately spotted the spectacular Milky Way and marveled at its size. The Milky Way, which is a barred spiral galaxy, stands out like a thirty-degree wide band of light, arching across the sky. It is a disk-like structure, with four spiral arms, when being viewed from within. Earth is said to be on the Orion Arm toward the outer part of the galaxy. Defying imagination, in the Milky Way alone it has been hypothesized there are 200 billion-to-400 billion stars, 100 billion planets, and a disk of gas and dust, called "interstellar medium," surrounding these entities. Furthermore, astronomers have suggested that everything in the Milky Way is moving at a velocity of 600 kilometers per second, or 373 miles per second. I couldn't quite wrap my mind around that. The ancients believed that if you listened hard enough you, you could almost hear the alleged harmonic energy of the movement of the heavenly bodies, the "music of the spheres." Assuming you could actually "hear" something, I imagined the sound would be deep, heavy, and mechanical, no harps.

I could have stayed out, watching, absorbing, becoming one with this indescribable scene, but Faust was becoming antsy and wanted to explore. He wasn't as hypnotized by the view above as I was. Furthermore, the temperature was dropping. I suggested to him that we snuggle in the sleeping bag, but that didn't fly. As I opened the sleeping bag, he oozed out of my grip. I could hear him thinking as he looked around, "Aw, gee, Mom, we could do this anytime. There's stuff out here to discover."

I've never been a religious person but the spirituality of the magnitude of the dome above us moved me. This was for me the truest feeling of being at one with the universe. It gave me a dose of humility. Feeling so small and insignificant, yet so full of wonder, made me a child again when I first discovered mature trees, the ocean, and mountainous formations. That must have been how ancient astronomers with their rudimentary telescopes felt when they first explored the glorious unexpected of the heavens.

Faust kept sniffing and straining on his leash to see what life might be out there lurking in the dark. Maybe a rabbit, lizard, or scorpion to chase or play with. That was until he heard a high-pitched cheeping-like whistle sound. It seemed to be coming noiselessly closer though I couldn't tell how far away it was. There wasn't much sound-dampening in the desert. Faust seemed intrigued. I thought, Be careful what you wish for. Then he looked slightly confused. Should he investigate or panic? It sounded like a bird ... but not. As it turned out, if he lived out there in the open, he would have learned early on to be afraid, very afraid of it.

What he didn't know, I had earlier discovered in a pamphlet on the area's wildlife, was that it was a much larger cat, one that out-weighed him by at least one hundred thirty pounds, that was on the prowl for an appetizer, entrée, or dessert. Faust wouldn't even have been an antipasto for this cat. I resentfully, but rapidly, gathered the sleeping bag and slung Faust over my shoulder and trotted inside. Unless the mountain lion were extremely hungry, it might not have come anywhere near where people were congregating. But, then again, if the cougar knew of Faust's notoriety, it might have risked it. As a result, it could have had bragging rights: "I had the world-famous Dancing Cat for brunch."

20

SCOTTY'S CASTLE UNDERCOVER

B right and early the next morning we started our journey to Scotty's Castle. Like almost everything else, it was a l-o-n-g forty-five miles from Stove Pipe Wells to its location in the Grapevine Canyon in Grapevine Mountains. Ironically, Scotty's Castle was not owned by anyone named Scott or Scotty. I knew that at least. What I didn't know was that it was the two-story, 32,000 square-foot vacation home of insurance millionaire couple Albert and Bessie Johnson. When I was a child, I had seen a Charlie Chan movie about a castle in the desert that was suggestive of Scotty's castle—well, in a Hollywood re-imagining of it anyway.

In 1922 the Johnsons designed it as an odd mixture of Mission Revival and Spanish Colonial Revival, with European ironwork, hand-hewn beams, colorful Mexican tiles covering the kitchen sink and backsplash, stove, fireplaces, and terra-cotta octagonal saltillo tiles on the floors. Carved wood was everywhere from the kitchen cabinets, dining room built-in shelves, to the curved ceiling of the Upper Music Room, to the second-floor railings which ran around the perimeter of the living room below.

European-style tapestries, some of which I thought perhaps might be copies of late-medieval and Renaissance weavings like those found in the Art Institute of Chicago, hung below the railings for decoration and perhaps insulation as well on cold desert nights. Sofas and chairs were high-backed leather. Tiffany lamps abounded. Two-tiered octagonal wrought-iron chandeliers hung throughout providing an alpenglow ambiance. A nearby spring about three hundred feet above the house was used to generate electricity. And by allowing the water to drip over a constructed rock face in the Great Hall, it also provided air-conditioning of sorts through evaporative cooling.

Outside as we all gathered to take the castle tour, a heavy-set woman with a red beret and black skirt gave us a cheerfully brief history of the castle. Then, before we entered, she pointed to an alcove and told us where to put our food and drinks. "Oh, and if you're have gum or anything else in your mouth, deposit it in the trash can here," pointing to a hidden receptacle. No kidding. If even lozenge-sucking wasn't permissible, you can bet a cat wouldn't be permissible either.

Obviously, I couldn't put him back in the car unless instant heat prostration was an acceptable result. I sidled silently away from the group, pulled the knapsack off my shoulders, and carefully folded the knapsack's fabric top flap, which I had never employed with Faust, slightly over his head, still leaving him plenty of room to see and breathe.

We entered through a heavy, red, elaborately-carved wood door with long, black wrought-iron straps. Once we were inside the building, Faust contented himself to stay mostly hidden, quietly spying from his knapsack. He only stuck his nose out from under the flap to occasionally pivot his head to take in the complexity of colors, sounds, and smells. I was pleased that as far as I could tell he wasn't attempting to lean out to playfully rearrange the expensive knickknacks, which were abundant, with a swipe of his paw.

So, who was Scotty and why was it called *his* castle? The story goes that Scotty, whose name was Walter E. Scott, had been a trick rider with William Frederick "Buffalo Bill" Cody's Wild West Show, a long-time con artist, gold prospector of sorts, and a teller of great tales. After approaching Albert Johnson with a "have I got a great deal for you" proposal, he talked Johnson into investing $4,000 in his "gold mine." Johnson liked Scott. However, over time when Scott kept finding excuses for never providing the gold he claimed to have mined as promised, Johnson finally discovered the mine was a fraud, not just played out but non-existent. Yet, surprisingly, in spite of this, Johnson enjoyed Scotty's magnetic stories and his company so much that he kept him around to entertain him and his guests.

He built quarters for Scotty both at the castle and at a five-room cabin at Lower Vine Ranch, some distance from the castle. It was replete with outbuildings and a corral for Scotty's beloved mules. When the Johnsons weren't in residence, they paid Scotty to act as caretaker of the ranch. Later, after the Johnsons died, Scotty lived at the castle until his own death in 1954. Not a bad deal for a con artist-turned-celebrated raconteur.

Faust had been playing the perfect guest until we arrived at our last point of interest on the tour, the Upper Music Room, located on the second floor. The room was long and large and decked out in opulent red and gold. Overhead there were what appeared to be dozens of hand-carved, curved, and scalloped beams in redwood which were highlighted by the same large two-tiered, wrought-iron, multi-light octagonal chandeliers that distinguished the living room. In the center of the room were comfortable 1920s' chairs arranged in a conversational grouping. To the right was a large "semi-curved" fireplace. There was also a hand-painted copy of Raphael's "Madonna della Sedia" on the wall's surface.

To the left was an alcove on a raised platform, with a grand piano, backed by a fancy carved wooden screen. On its far wall was a magical control panel. This was where an incredible 1,121-pipe Welte-Mignon pipe organ player system was set up to play four hundred different rolls of the Johnsons' favorite music. If you wanted to hear piano, organ, glockenspiel, xylophone, bells of all kinds, chimes, drums and cymbals, and a calliope, it was all there waiting for you with a simple flip of the right switches. The acoustics in the vaulted room were dynamic. Reflective and absorptive surfaces of the room were apparently designed to provide good and pleasant sound coverage. The music filled every room crevice.

However, when the tour director played a roll of calliope music, Faust started to stir. It must have reminded him of the music he heard when we visited the Palace Playland amusement park in Old Orchard Beach, Maine. That morning we were deluged with torrential rain under black skies. While we didn't get the opportunity to ride their world-famous carousel, the Ferris wheel, or have saltwater taffy, we did enjoy hearing the carousel's calliope music drift from across the street to the parking lot as the rain violently pummeled our car there.

With that reminder, Faust now began to shift in his knapsack, his feet once again pushing against my back. I could feel him elbow me as his forearms moved to ascend toward the knapsack's narrow opening. No sooner had he begun to do that than the castle's interior tour had to be over for us. Before we could examine the three-keyboard organ itself at the end of the room, where organ concerts were held, I began to back quietly out of the room. This was just as the tour guide selected another roll of music to play. Down the stairs, we were out of there.

Before we checked out the stables, cook house, "Hacienda" (guest house), four wrought-iron-filigreed red wood main gates, the large Music Room Tower with its spiral staircase leading to outside the Upper Music Room, the clock and chimes tower with its two-octave carillon which played Westminster chime ever quarter-hour, and the pool that the Johnsons never finished, I rolled down the car windows a little to let out some of the accumulated heat and then started the car's air-conditioner. It would take fifteen minutes before the car would be habitable again, even in March. We then saw nearly all there was to see. Amazing.

Next on our agenda was the Racetrack Playa where boulders occasionally moved along a dry lake bed. Much to my chagrin the Racetrack was over thirty-three miles from the castle. From the Racetrack to the seven-hundred-and-fifty-foot-deep volcanic Ubehebe Crater was another twenty-seven miles. Good grief! That was sixty miles! And that wasn't even counting the drive back to Stovepipe Wells. Faust and I took a welcomed water break before starting on the road again.

While I certainly wasn't expecting everything to be arranged in close proximity like at Disneyland, I was finding all this driving on slow gravely roads with long distances between attractions an increasing pain. I mean, this place was natural and fascinating but … Besides, I wasn't sure Faust was actually enjoying its natural uniqueness as much as I was. We left for the Racetrack and maybe we'd stop by the crater, and maybe not.

The Racetrack Playa was the opposite of Badwater Basin in altitude, at 3,700 feet *above* sea level. It was an exceptionally flat and level plane created by an influx of sediment. When the rains roared down from the nearby mountains, they flooded the plane, drying it to soft thick mud which cracked into a mosaic pattern of interlocking polygons. That was neat. And nary a piece of vegetation existed on it. That was hard to believe given how tenacious some native, harsh-environment seeds could be in surviving anyplace there was soil and a touch of precipitation. It wasn't much to look at except for some trails etched on the surface by the "mysterious" moving boulders.

The explanation of the movement of the dolomite and syenite, an igneous rock that looks something like granite, boulders was that when there was a thin ice sheet on the surface which had started to melt, slight winds could push the boulders along the surface, up to five meters a minute. That was an astounding fact. However, as Faust and I walked and walked the playa, getting our exercise, nothing was melting or moving. After Faust sniffed the ground, the cracks, and a boulder, he looked at me as if to say, "Yeah, so? Now what?" I had to agree with him. I wanted to *see* something spectacular, not just *know* it could happen. Still, I was glad I had taken a look. After trudging along the lake bed, I felt touristed out.

After the racetrack, I couldn't conjure up enough motivation to check out the Ubehebe Crater. The large volcanic crater, a half-mile across, was created by a steam and gas explosion. This resulted when hot magma rose from the depths, reached ground water, and created steam pressure detonation. The walk around the rim was one and a half miles with loose footing due to the cinder layer. The difficulty of seeing it was in the initial steep climb to the rim. Not today. It would have to wait for another time.

21

CAMPING SURPRISES

It was back to Stove Pipe Wells, with a return trip to Mesquite Flat Sand Dunes. Even without my hiking boots, we walked and walked and Faust scanned every hummock on foot. No native critters revealed themselves. There would be no fun encounters after all. After that disappointment and his constantly having to successively shake each paw of sand, he quickly tired of slogging through the dunes' deep, loose granularity. Oh, well. Back to the cabin for another night.

The next morning around eight o'clock I dressed in hiking boots and cargo pants and took a jacket for our day of camping out. I had reserved a spot at Mahogany Flat campground because it was located in groupings of juniper trees. Furthermore, it was at the start of the Telescope Peak hiking trail which I thought Faust and I might try.

Like everything else in Death Valley, it was another long haul to reach it. But it was a clear, sunny day and Faust and I had slept well. In a good mood, I accepted the sixty-mile jaunt with good grace. My grandmother, my mother's mother, used to say, "There can be no beauty without pain." Philosophically, I was never quite sure what she meant but somehow it seemed to apply. Travel was warm and slow but Faust, who was curled around my shoulders, took it in stride, scanning the terrain, I assumed, for wildlife, the flying and ground-hugging kind.

After fifty-seven miles, a sign welcoming us to Mahogany Flat indicated that the campground was a mere three miles up a dirt road. Great! We're almost there! I was looking forward to pitching our Eureka tent and starting up the hiking trail. I could see Faust, who was now perched on the passenger seat staring out the window, hopping from one rear leg to another, getting excited as we approached a copse of junipers. "Yes, Faust," I laughed, "we'll be able to get out and explore in just a few minutes."

We hadn't gone thirty feet before the dirt road turned into a path of two, parallel, car-width, three-foot-deep ruts. Oh, crap! I pounded the steering wheel. This required high clearance and the navigation capability of a four-by-four. Had this been broadcast? How had I missed that very pertinent piece of information? Damn! Damn! Damn! There was no way my rented Honda Accord was going to be able to accept this challenge.

With no one behind me, I carefully began to back up. Screwing my head over my right shoulder to do this was threatening to put my trapezius muscles into spasm. Back at the sign, I surveyed the land around us, shaking my head at my error. I'd already paid for the camping site and wasn't interested in retracing my steps back to Stove Pipe Wells in order to locate another nearby site. We'd just come almost sixty miles, for crying out loud. Besides, from the pictures I had viewed of the available campgrounds, Mahogany appeared to be the only one with any trees and a little privacy. The others unapologetically offered flat gravely open areas surrounded by nearby tents and motorized campers. That held zero appeal. It definitely wasn't my idea of camping in the wild.

If I could avoid the fence post to the right, I might be able to manage to pull over onto the embankment on the right without getting the car's undercarriage hung up. I looked at Faust, "What do you say? Should we give it a go?" He looked back and crawled over onto my shoulders again. I took that as a vote of confidence. There was a slight sound of scraping before we attained the embankment. From there we paralleled the road for about a mile, dodging shrubs and trees, then parked in a small, somewhat hidden space under several trees when we couldn't drive any further. I knew we were illegal but hoped the park rangers wouldn't patrol the area and ticket us.

The yellow and green tent required arching Fiberglas poles to give it its semi-circular shape. Knowing I was in for a battle with the physics of straight poles fighting being bent as they slipped through small narrow fabric tent loops, I had left Faust in the car with the air-conditioner running. I hurried, talking to God as I struggled. When our desert dome was finally up and staked, I threw the sleeping bag, change of clothing, camp stove, fuel, and chow inside, zipped it closed, and turned off the car. Filling my cargo pants pockets with a compass, snake bite kit, a small roll of bandages, utility knife, mirror, matches, and whistle, I hoped I was being prepared for possible contingencies. With a jacket wrapped around my waist, a water canteen attached to my belt, and Faust wrapped around my neck on top of his knapsack, we started the two-mile trek to the campground and the Telescope Peak's trailhead. Even though it had been eighty-two degrees at Stove Pipe Wells, now at an elevation of over 8,000 feet, it was getting cooler. As we climbed Telescope Peak, it would get cooler still.

At the trailhead I found I was more tired than I had expected from walking on the rocky, uneven ground along the road. The elevation didn't help either. Faust and I whetted our whistles as I read more signage. It explained that the trail was thirteen miles long, with no available water on the way. Hikers should expect it to take seven to nine hours. What? As I looked up the steep, rough, zig-zagging trail, I could see why. This was not like hiking in Massachusetts or New Hampshire. I hadn't brought a wooden staff, ski pole, much less a collapsible trekking pole, which I'd need for balance on the trail. Good move.

I wanted to hike this trail because I was particularly interested in seeing bristlecone pines which braved growing on the cold, windy Telescope Peak. But it was beginning to look as though we weren't going to see any of these ancient, gale-twisted, almost-needle-less trees after all. I'd seen photos of the so-called "Methuselah tree" in *National Geographic* and wanted to examine them up-close to appreciate their persistence and tenacity. At five thousand years old, they were among some of the longest living life forms on the earth. Incredibly resilient, they have been battered by harsh weather at high elevations in the worst of soils. Yet they have not only hung on but also thrived.

I wondered if maybe the harshness they had adapted to and accommodated was the secret to their longevity. That was a concept the implications of which was something I didn't want to think about. I believed to a degree that what doesn't kill us makes us stronger, but there was a limit. I would adapt and accommodate where I had to but I wasn't going to seek out "harshness" if that's what it took to increase longevity. There was plenty of it already naturally occurring to deal with without making oneself a "bring-it-on" masochist.

With Faust in his knapsack and me in my jacket we started up the trail. The altitude at the trailhead didn't seem to bother me particularly but as we slowly ascended, I was beginning to feel a headache coming on. I thought it was too soon—we were only at a little above eighty-one-hundred feet—for altitude sickness to affect me. I was in good shape from running my forty-plus miles a week. But this was slow going. My calves and thighs were beginning to burn as a result of the steepness of the climb and the canting of the rough trail. I felt like such a wash-out.

Faust was scanning the terrain from under the bill of the baseball cap I wore backwards to protect him from the intense sun. The sun was already starting to scorch my sunscreen-deficient nose. I knew I had forgotten something. Every so often I stopped to take in the scenery and catch my breath. It wasn't long before I began to stop frequently. The next time I surveyed the nearby mountains, I glimpsed a mule deer grazing on another peak. I pointed it out to Faust who was busy looking toward the ground. I'm not sure he actually spotted the deer. Inspecting all that was immediately around him, he appeared to hope we'd encounter some wildlife he could chase. Maybe even a squirrel would do. On second thought, it shouldn't be a squirrel. It might remind him of his frustrating backyard exploits with "Rooster." And who knew what he'd do then.

The pinyon pines, junipers, and mahogany that were so prevalent at the trailhead were quickly disappearing as we slogged our way upward. Because it was early Spring, there were still patches of snow here and there amid the scrub along the sides of the rocky trail. The peak had more snow. If it had been later in the season, we might have seen desert wildflowers and cacti in bloom on the alpine grasslands … if we could reach that far. From the top of Telescope Peak we would have been presented with a glorious three-hundred-sixty-degree view of California and Nevada, seeing hundreds of miles in all directions.

The more I huffed and puffed, the more my legs cramped,

and the worse my headache became. I had no idea of our elevation at that time. Boy, I wasn't prepared for this. Running did not do it. At the rate I was going I knew we were unlikely to do little more than a mile ... maybe two if we were very lucky. Suddenly it occurred to me. If I were having difficulty breathing, how was Faust doing with his weakened lungs.

I stopped on the side of the trail and slipped off his knapsack to look at him. He had his mouth open, panting. His chest was working hard and fast, moving air in and out of his lungs. Damn! I slapped my forehead with the heel of my hand. I should have been watching him more carefully. When I checked now and then, he seemed to be interested in everything around him. But now it was obvious that he wasn't at his best, much less having a great time. Guilt was strangling me as I started to tear up. "Okay, kiddo," I croaked, "I think that's enough for the day. How about we head back to the tent and have a little rest and something to eat?"

He didn't respond. He looked semi-conscious and a little glassy-eyed. The trip down was faster but it was harder to keep my balance as my boots tripped and rolled over the rock shards, upsetting my balance. By the time we reached the trailhead again, and sat in the shade of a juniper, Faust looked a little better but not as I felt he should. We had some water. He lapped slowly out of the handled steel cup that I'd attached to my canteen for him. After I staggered two miles back to the tent, he lay down on my sleeping bag. I found him a small can of soft food. He casually whiffed the contents but chose to nap for a while instead of eating. I monitored him for a while until he seemed to be breathing normally.

As he snoozed, I read more of the newest Robin Cook novel which was becoming more predictable by the page. I'd been collecting Cook's works for years but this recent one was like the last, another disappointment. His characters were becoming more two-dimensional. I couldn't relate to or empathize with the protagonist. And the story's premise struck me as absurd. I should have brought Sue Grafton's latest alphabet mystery series book instead. Her protagonist, Kinsey Millhone, a private investigator, was full-fledged and identifiable, as were the other colorful characters, and the plots were unusual, intricate, and well-wrought.

When Faust woke up, he looked better, even perky. It was time for a shoulder scritch session. Between his free-floating clavicles was his special place. As he sinuously moved his body around in response to my touch, his heading bobbing and tongue flicking as if he were licking his upper foreleg, I heard something outside the tent. It was like a clicking or the rapid movement of dry leaves. Oddly, the first thing that came to mind was a Salvation Army band member rapidly shaking a tambourine. Since the flap was already unzipped, I left Faust and crawled over to the opening and quietly peered out. Not fifteen feet from us was what looked like a long-tailed, long-beaked, spotted, scrawny chicken. It was a roadrunner! No kidding. It had something long, dangling, and moving in its beak. OMG! It was a rattler!

We were close to it! What should I do? I thought I'd zip up the flap. But the noise or movement could startle the roadrunner which might then drop the live snake. That could be very awkward. Maybe I should wait to see how successful the feathered predator would be. If the bird dropped its prey somewhat farther away from the tent, I could always zip up the flap ASAP just in case.

As I pondered what to do, Faust, who was no longer enjoying his due, quietly edged beside me to join me in looking out. The bird, which was holding the limbless reptile by its head, worked at shaking it as the nearly two-foot-long snake writhed.

With his ears forward and eyes squinting, Faust began to creep over the edge of the tent toward the roadrunner. I grabbed his harness. The snake's movements finally ceased and the bird, hop-skipping, dragged it away. But Faust really wanted to follow the bird to investigate. His galloping front paws shoveled the gritty soil back at me, into the tent, as he strained to follow the cartoonish movements of the departing bird.

Ooh, rattlers. Their presence did not provide solace. Even though I had saved rattlers on several occasions—once when one got stuck trying to go through a chicken wire fence and the other, when it was sleeping on the warm road with a car approaching—the fact that there was one obvious rattler where we planned to sleep tonight could indicate that it had siblings, mates, or progeny possibly slithering around there too. I was sure Faust and I weren't really in any danger. Snakes do try to avoid humans whenever possible. But there was always the possibility of one inching its way under the tent for warmth. Suddenly camping here didn't feel seductive any longer.

After carefully surveying the ground around us, I attached Faust's leash to his harness and tied it to a tent stake. Faust was languidly stretching, sharpening his claws on the trunk of a nearby juniper as I hurried to the car to inspect it everywhere, even under the hood and in its wheel wells. No snakes!

Whoa! I slapped my forehead again. What did I just do? Ye gods and little fishes! I'd left Faust outside! That was a dumb place to leave him. Why was I leaving? Because of rattlers! And I'd tied him out in the open where he's be defenseless if another were seeking retaliation for the roadrunner's caper.

I quickly retrieved him and secured his leash to the door handle in the back seat. He looked at me surprised. After I turned on the car's engine and air-conditioner, I started removing everything from the tent, taking it down, re-packing the trunk and back seat. Once I'd finished, I untied Faust and wrapped him around my shoulders again.

Turning around was not the piece of cake I imagined. The way I'd parked nose-in in this small space required me to turn the wheel to the left and slowly back up, turn the wheel to the right and pull forward, and repeat that process until the nose of the car was pointing toward the campground entrance.

We slowly drove back to the welcome sign, carefully navigated re-crossing the embankment, with more undercarriage scraping, then headed back to Stove Pipe Wells. We had the cabin for one more day. On the return Faust seemed content to stare out the windshield. I think he was disappointed his brief hunting foray had been curtailed but he hid it well. He rarely pouted. But when he did, it wasn't for long, only long enough to get his point across to sometimes-dull-witted humans.

22

SIN CITY BECKONS

I was feeling unaccountably restless as we drove back. Maybe, I thought, we should leave and drive back by way of the 280-mile long Grand Canyon. I wanted us to see it sometime and this seemed like a good time, but ... that was three hundred and seventy-five miles from where we were, another six hours of driving. Besides, I'd want to do more than view it from the South and North rims. I'd read about hiking the 9.5-mile Bright Angel Trail, which had its trailhead at Grand Canyon Village. It was a difficult, steep hike with sweeping switchbacks, requiring a trekking pole, like Telescope Peak. The elevation drop from the rim to Phantom Ranch at the bottom was 4,450 feet.

There were two rest houses along the way, "One-and-a-Half Mile" and "Three-Mile." So the shortest walk would be three miles total, down and back. But I had read that the rule of thumb was that if hiking down to whatever location took you an hour, hiking back up would take two hours. Considering how much hotter and drier it became as one descended, and how I'd have to be concerned about dehydration and salt replacement for Faust and me, I felt that likewise didn't sound all that appealing. My headache was receding slightly but something was wrong. Well, not "wrong" exactly but somewhat amiss.

Maybe we could drive west to Sequoia National Park to see those spectacular giants. I imagined being surrounded by groves of the world's largest living life forms, standing among them, the relative size of a mushroom spore molecule by comparison. Faust would no doubt want to attempt to climb these challenging trees. That was not something either the park rangers or I would have relished. Poor Faust. This wasn't his day for unfettered freedom to explore.

The California map I'd bought when we arrived at Death Valley showed the circuitous route to Sequoia. First, we'd have to drive south to California City then north again, for a total of two hundred sixty-eight miles. That was at least four and one-half hours once you drove west to leave Death Valley. Damn! Still, if we went there, we could also go to Kings Canyon National Park, which was adjacent to Sequoia. I had read that John Muir once stated that Kings Canyon, which has mountains, caverns, and is the home of America's deepest canyon, was a "rival to Yosemite." That was inviting.

But no matter how inviting that sounded I was running out of spit. I realized I was trying to do too much in a short period of time, even though we had three weeks. Three weeks?

Thinking I could fill three weeks with tourism was a version of insanity. So far, our vacation was feeling more like a contest of endurance than a relaxing sojourn. Back at the cabin I called the airline to see if I could change our return flight. Amazingly, I could, which I'm sure would never happen again without my incurring a hefty penalty. We stayed our last night in the cabin and in the morning started for Las Vegas but not until we met some locals.

Standing up ahead in the middle of the road was a group of the "trespassing" burros which were found throughout the backcountry. They seemed oblivious to the car approaching. Among them was a small youngster, all fuzzy gray with black ears, a white muzzle, eye ring, and belly, a short black mane, and a black stripe running down its back which was intersected perpendicularly by another black stripe at its shoulders. The resulting cross on its back was probably why some called this critter a "Bethlehem burro."

It looked like the burro my grandfather had had when I was a child, one he had later foisted upon us when he wanted to get rid of it. We were in Pennsylvania at the time, renting the caretaker's cottage on a country club estate which had stables and a corral that our three horses used. So "Tamale" the burro would fit right in. She was never friendly, though I had hoped my petting her and lavishing attention on her would change that. Since she had survived "granddaddy dearest" in one piece, she may have just wanted to be left alone, to exist untrammeled, except for occasionally nipping at the horses' rear ends to show who was boss.

When the group didn't move or respond to my beeping the horn, I drove a little closer. They looked at me, unconcerned. I stopped the car, got out, and cautiously walked toward them. I have no idea what possessed me to think I was a wild-ass wrangler. Faust was on the dashboard, his body hugging the windshield, trying to get as close as possible to these large, unusual animals.

The baby was standing in the center of their loosely arranged circle. But as I neared, it walked over to me. I petted its head and back and tried to give it a gentle push toward the side of the road. It nearly toppled over, being wobbly on its young legs. I could hear Faust mohwing loudly, frenetically. He didn't want to be left out of this encounter.

The other burros started walking toward me too, looking curious, perhaps hoping I had something delectable to eat. You could tell they loved park visitors. With wishful thinking, I encouraged them to follow me to the side of the road which they took their own sweet time doing. Once they were out of my path, I slowly moved forward. Fake out. Sorry.

Oh, how I wanted to take the baby with me. The park would probably have liked me to take the whole gang since the burros were an invasive species, not native to North America. Sadly, they unintentionally damaged the ecosystem and competed with native wildlife, like bighorn sheep and desert tortoises, for the limited vegetative resources. After our delightful chance meeting, I found I felt a little uplifted. The drive back didn't seem like such a chore any longer.

As we drove along I-95 toward Las Vegas, a black, semi-tractor, maybe a Kenworth, with a long, sloped squared-off hood, stormed up behind me to ride my bumper. Not again! This had happened to me once before, years ago, when I was driving north from San Diego to Fullerton on I-5 to Rt. 90. That tractor trailer likewise rode my bumper giving me a bad time, like in the 1971 movie "Duel," which was based on the Richard Matheson short story.

In the film a terrified motorist driving a Plymouth Valiant is being stalked upon remote and lonely California canyon roads by the mostly unseen driver of an unkempt 1955 Peterbilt 281 tanker truck with a long hood and split windscreen. The motorist first encounters the tanker truck on a two-lane highway in the Mojave Desert while the trucker is traveling just below the speed limit, expelling sooty diesel exhaust. When the motorist passes the truck, the truck suddenly roars past him, blasting its horn at him. This trucker's cat-and-mouse game continues until it is obvious that the trucker wants to kill the motorist … and tries his best to do so. Fortunately, my experience wasn't that extreme.

I had been minding my own business, in the right lane exceeding the speed limit, on my way to California State University Fullerton to meet a psych. professor when a tractor trailer roared up behind me. I saw it in my rearview mirror and thought it was going to crash into me. It slowed just in time but continued to tailgate me. At one point it tapped the back of my 1960s two-tone green Ford sedan. I couldn't see its license plate if it had one. Since its bumper and mine didn't match, I assumed it had inflicted some damage around the trunk area when it kissed my car's rear.

Acrid sweat was oozing, dripping, wafting in the hot summer air inside the un-air-conditioned car. Despite my Mitchum's deodorant, I was soon smelling like raw onions. Suddenly the semi zoomed past and slid right in front of me, its rear just missing my hood. My brain screamed at me, "If he's trying to kill you, you are dead meat!" I pulled out and rammed the accelerator to the floor boards. My old car balked for a second then grabbed hold of the road. Approaching my cut-off to N. Placentia Avenue and the campus in a quarter mile, I zoomed past the truck.

I caught only a glimpse of the trucker above me. He was wearing reflective sun glasses and a John Deere cap with the bill pulled low, shadowing his face. As I passed, he gave me a malevolent grin. I was scared ... and nonplussed. I didn't understand what was going on. Why he was being so aggressive. I hadn't done anything to him. Maybe he'd seen the film and thought this competition would be macho fun, especially with a female at the wheel of the car on the momentarily quiescent highway. Maybe he was psychotic. Maybe he was high on something. I exited my off ramp, soaked, heart hammering, and very confused.

Later, after I'd reached CSUF and had calmed down a little, I found I wanted to laugh. In my hovering anxiety a strange thought had occurred to me. If this had been part of an Alfred Hitchcock movie, Bernard Herrmann, who orchestrated the music for most of Hitchcock's films, would have used similar energetic, chaotic, fandango dance music he had used in the intro to *North by Northwest* to accompany my inexplicable death-defying experience. If only I drank, I really could have used a shot of something strong and neat right then.

Faust had missed all the melodrama with the truck. Fortunately, the driver apparently had tired of the game and passed me, likely exceeding ninety miles per hour. I thanked the Fates that he hadn't blasted his air horn and scared Faust nearly to death.

Taking our time, we made it back to Las Vegas by early afternoon. I thought we ought to look around to see what everyone raved about. We drove through town to look at the casinos. Traffic was faster than I'd have imagined. I thought we'd just poke along. Without all the flashing lights against a black sky, the so-called glitter of this famous town looked merely garish in the sunshine. Rubbernecking, I saw there were no parking spaces to be had along the then four-point-two-mile "Strip," South Las Vegas Boulevard. The first thing we saw was the iconic neon sign with a big star, "Welcome to Fabulous Las Vegas Nevada," which serves as the unofficial welcome mat to this gambling mecca. We drove down one side of the street than up the other side to see all we could see. In truth, it was hard to spot anything to get a full impression. Finally, we found a restaurant of sorts and had lunch. We dawdled, looking at a map of the city, checking what other sights there might be.

As silly as it sounded, I wanted to do something wild and adventuresome with Faust. He had been showing me what life could be like without my social anxiety. That risks were not only necessary but also could be fun. Mulling it over, I suddenly had an aha! What if I took him to the front of one of these casinos where people were gathered on the sidewalk or apron and encouraged him to do one of his outstanding performances for everyone? Could I? Would I? Should I? For seven minutes I debated with myself. Would I get into trouble? Why should I? I had no intention of actually entering the casino. It would be unlikely to welcome a cat anyway. Besides, that kind of gambling wasn't for me. Living and trying to succeed in business was already enough of a gamble. So why the hell not?

Back on the Strip, we cruised up and down, making several loops until I spotted a casino and a main street parking lot near it on my right that cost ten bucks a pop. I whispered to Faust on my shoulders, "Do you want to go have some real fun?" He rubbed his face against my ear. With him still on my shoulders we parked, walked two blocks, and crossed the expansive casino parking lot to the east entrance of Circus Circus. This was the largest permanent big top in the world. The 1971 James Bond film, *Diamonds Are Forever*, was filmed in its Midway.

Talk about gaudy. Just like a carnival. There was a long, curved marquee over the entrance that was dotted with thousands of red lights, making its large name stand out. Under the marquee were thousands of close lines of yellow lights. These yellow lights also outlined arched areas on the building. Above the marquee was a stripped tent-like roof with yellow lights running along the length of the stripes. All lights were aglow. It was at this entrance that tour buses dropped off and picked up their guests. A bus had just unloaded a tour. People were mingling, checking locations of what the casino offered, and chatting before entering.

As I hesitantly approached, I patted Faust, whispering, "Are you ready?" After a minute or so, my heart leaping out of chest, I got up the gumption to ask loudly, "May I have your attention?" People turned their heads, perhaps wondering if I were associated with the casino. "I'd like to introduce to you Faust the Dancing Cat." I took him off my shoulders and placed him about three feet in front of them. "Can anyone here hum the 'Blue Danube Waltz'?" A number of people looked quizzical while others appeared either not to have heard me or thought it was a Candid Camera prank and feared being made fun of. "Okay," I said, swallowing hard, "I'll start."

I squeakily hummed a few bars and Faust started to waltz. I was awaiting my heart attack. Slowly curiosity began to ripple toward those in back who moved closer to see what was going on. In his first few steps Faust had them. I quickly added, "Since we don't have actual accompaniment, please imagine the lilting strains of Strauss's orchestral melody as background as he continues to glide through his routine. Maybe you could join me in humming the melody for him?"

Pacing himself as the group hummed, he rolled over, walked on his back legs for four feet, then did a hand stand. More people joined in the hum fest as he walked up my legs backwards, lay on his back to juggle a ball I gave him. When he walked around and through my legs as I jauntily sauntered under the marquee, they cheered. When he backflipped, somersaulted, and finished by jumping onto my shoulders where he curled up, the applause was thunderous and long.

There was one stunt that I didn't signal Faust to do before this audience. It was a front flip. When I hadn't offered him my linked hands as a platform for it, he thankfully didn't attempt it. The ongoing problem with accomplishing that feat was that while he could get himself into the air and vertical with his head down, he couldn't follow through with the flip. Instead, he'd twist his body back into a regular forward leap. Maybe he'd accomplish it one day but I wasn't so sure about that.

Irrespective, Faust, basking in the glory of his celebrity, jumped down from my shoulders to allow his captivated audience to pet him, which they did. He was in his element. I was proud of him and so happy for him, especially as they took up a chant of "More! More!"

"Oh, my! I can't believe he did that!" stated several older people. "That was wonderful. Thank you!"

"Amazing! I didn't know you could train cats. How in the world did you train him to do all that?" questioned numbers of others.

"I'd love to see another performance with real music and all. Does he do his act here?" asked another group of individuals as they scanned their Circus Circus information sheets. They nodded, "I hope so."

He had done his full performance, dancing his heart out, and presenting his acrobatics repertoire to date, to their oohs and ahs and broad grins. With his whiskers up, amber eyes glinting, and vampire teeth revealed, Faust savored their acclamation as he continued to receive accolades. Just then a uniformed man appeared at the entrance door and pushed his way through. I guessed he might have been a concierge since I had viewed him striding from the hall leading to the Midway. I suddenly felt my heart skip a beat or two. Was he trying to determine why there was an unmoving mass of humanity at the entrance, and clapping, but not spending their tourist money inside where they should be. He took one look at me and frowned, stating, "No cats allowed! Only service animals for the disabled are allowed in here."

"Not a problem," I replied, trying to smile, my heart tripping again. Hastily I scooped Faust back onto my shoulders. We'd already achieved our goal. And I'd made it without cardiac arrest or bowing out.

Someone asked, "But doesn't this talented cat work here?

He really should. He has a great act."

As numbers of people paused to lean over to give Faust a final pat on the head and thank him, the man, who was now looking slightly disgruntled at their behavior, rapidly pasted a smile on his face to welcome the tour in with open arms. He then had them follow him inside to the Midway carnival where they could lighten their wallets.

Gleaming with pride, we made our way back to the car. If it hadn't been for Faust's ongoing high sense of adventure, that sort of public thing might never have occurred to me. Moreover, I'd likely have been too concerned about being negatively evaluated to have had the chutzpah to try it. It was crazy … but what the hey … it was fun! Consequently, afterward if anyone asked about Faust's national renown, I was ready to say nonchalantly, "Why, yes, Faust has even played Vegas! He wowed them at Circus Circus." Unfortunately, no one ever asked. But we knew and that was all that really mattered.

We had our flight reservation for early the next morning. We stopped at the same restaurant for a repeat of taco salad, with chicken for Faust, and the motel that had saved us on the way in. Yes, once again, they had a room that was free of a urine-soaked towel. We spent the rest of the day lounging and playing. Sleep came quickly that night and we slept like the dead, feeling fully revived the next morning. I hadn't realized how stressed I must have been.

As we were winging our way back home, happily there was no repeat of the traumatic bathroom incident. In fact, the only untoward happening was when an obese male passenger in coach in front of us dropped a roast beef sandwich he had brought with him. Instantaneously, Faust, who had been sniffing the air and salivating from the moment the stranger had unwrapped it, leapt off my lap to snag it before the man could retrieve it from the floor. I grabbed it from Faust who already had one of his vampire fangs into a good-sized piece of meat from it. Then I tapped the passenger on the back as he was struggling to bend over and handed the sandwich back to him. I don't think he could have seen the robbery take place. And he didn't seem to notice what was missing. He grunted "thanks" then ... he *resumed eating it.* Ooh, icky! My gag reflex exercised itself. Faust, on the other hand, had his mouth full of beef. I didn't think he cared where it might have been. He chewed contentedly as he crawled back onto my lap, dragging the rest of the piece with him.

Back in Boston we duplicated the travel process in reverse, going to the bus, to the train, to a cab to get home. I was exhausted. As I unpacked, Faust just curled up on his favorite office chair. Looking very Cheshire Cat-ish, with a tiny piece of gristle hanging from his cheek, he took a nap. If only I could relax that way.

23

CHALLENGES

Life resumed without any momentous hitches. Faust was trying new acrobatic movements, mostly from watching people and animals on television. His front flip wasn't progressing. But it seemed like his repertoire still was increasing exponentially as he worked on his new moves. He was learning to walk on a taut clothesline, jump through a barrel stay held high, balance on a beachball and roll it forward, roll the beachball in front of him, bow, and shake hands. He'd have to go to Hollywood to present himself on late night shows once he perfected them as well. I, on the other hand, was slowly acquiring more coaching clients, especially in self-promotion, marketing, communication, and networking. They were mostly from the Boston area and suburbs. I was also doing more speaking gigs.

One presentation in particular that was becoming popular was a slide show about what one could learn about marketing and persuasion from the Iran-Contra Hearings. That was fun because it involved describing in precise detail how Oliver

North's verbal and nonverbal interpersonal communication techniques while testifying had cleverly and significantly changed the public's perception of him. In fact, in a single day of testimony the publics' favorability rating of him rose from 6 percent to 43 percent.

What did North do to transform his image? Observing his testimony and taking notes, I discovered he used six basic image factors. *First,* he used his physical appearance. He was dressed in his perfectly-fitted, full-dress Marine uniform, resplendent with six rows of ribbons and one row of medals. He was a ram-rod straight, clean-shaven, with a regulation hair-cut, an honored Vietnam veteran. *Second,* he used his movements, gestures, facial expressions, voice inflection, and intonation to create the feeling for what he was to say. He leaned forward, elbows braced, hands clasped, chin raised, gaze direct, and brow furrowed. *Third,* he used verbal behavior. When he talked, he spoke slowly, deliberately, pausing to articulate points, and choosing words to reinforce the image he was creating. *Fourth,* he showed intimate involvement in whatever he said, whether it was a philosophical statement or impassioned soliloquy. Neither his conviction nor energy ever waned. *Fifth,* he used illustrations. He conveyed his narrative, point by point, through stories, analogies, characterizations, speeches, lectures, and props. *Sixth,* he controlled the image he wanted to present, what he said, how he said it, and what he used to support each point. Anything beyond that he didn't address. And the camera loved him. And so did Faust who enjoyed my slide show as well, seemingly held spellbound by North's projected emotional earnestness.

In conclusion, Oliver North saw the circumstances as an opportunity to market himself and get his personal message across. He was aware of his situation and the importance of image factors. He prepared to act. And he acted. As a result, over night he transformed himself for many from the image of a "swaggering messianic crook" to that of a "selfless, flag-wrapped Guardian of the Western Hemisphere." It makes me wonder what else he could have achieved if he had had even more theatrical air time. He was the Sir John Gielgud of the Congressional hearings.

Also, I was spending more time examining social anxiety, with which I was still suffering to a degree, with clinical researchers in the field. I was also coaching individuals with similar anxiety and phobic concerns. One of the revelations I helped others discover was that they had forbiddances which were based on loyalties and allegiances to early family members, their culture, and society that tended to guide their thoughts, beliefs, attitudes, emotions, and behavior, too often for ill. These were their *shoulds*.

One of my classic *shoulds* was that I should not do better than my father. Since he didn't succeed, I could not succeed because to do so was to be disloyal to him. Consequently, I tended to sabotage myself every time I was close to a success.

Soon social anxiety and interpersonal communication became the thrust of my coaching efforts and over a decade later led to my third book, *Diagonally-Parked in a Parallel Universe: Working Through Social Anxiety*. It was well-received and praised by therapists and leading clinical researchers in social anxiety and shyness. Through my own personal work, and using Faust as a risk-taking role model, I had *finally* managed *not* to sabotage that success! It was about time!

Six months went by uneventfully after our Spring trip to Death Valley. We were taking walks along the quiet road and inspecting the public land across the main drag. When Faust wasn't practicing new performance behaviors, he was exploring his yard in detail. He had taken up rock climbing the ledge behind his apple tree without a top rope, climbing harness, belay device, shoes, or helmet. Claws only. He also tried tight-rope walking along the rock wall on the other side of the house. However, his efforts to reach the pointed tops of the six-foot solid-board picket fence surrounding the property on three sides never reached fruition. The problem was grasping the sharp points such that he could pull his body to the top then find a place to balance. But, of course, he kept trying. A challenge is a challenge. And he was always up for a challenge.

One morning as we were sauntering around the grassy upper tier of the backyard, Faust almost met a mama raccoon which was shinnying down from the maple tree, at the top of the two stone steps, with her three youngsters. At the base of the tree when she saw Faust and me, she reared up with front paws outspread, upper lip curled exposing her sharp teeth, growling at us. Her kits looked at us curiously from behind her, testing the air, perhaps musing upon checking us out. Before they could try, I wrapped Faust's leash around my hand and began to back us away slowly.

Faust, however, seemed more inquisitive than afraid. As a result, he appeared disinclined to follow suit. Straining against his leash, he stood his ground. There was a good six feet between Faust and the mama. It was a Mexican standoff. She stared wide-eyed and he just looked back at her. Then, for some unknown reason, she settled down on all fours again, looking unafraid, and gathered her babies to her. Leisurely she waddled away toward the rear fence with her kits in single-file trailing behind her. She never looked back. We were lucky there was no physical interaction because mama could have made mincemeat of Faust.

Faust looked after them, his ears drooping. He seemed disappointed that she and the little ones had left. Did he think that maybe they could have gotten to know each other if given the chance? I was skeptical that it would have happened. But with Faust's apparent facility to communicate with other species maybe it wasn't really outside the realm of possibility.

24

THINGS CHANGE

One afternoon as I was brushing and smoothing Faust's short coat, my fingers detected that he felt thinner than I remembered. I had no idea of his exact age when I rescued him. It was only apparent that he wasn't a very young cat. Illness and starvation had blurred the lines of his chronology. My fingers explored his body carefully. Hmmm.

Yes, he seemed to be looking a little slimmer but nothing like how he looked when we first met. Then he was skeletal, a walking cadaver. I made a mental note to myself to keep an eye on him: his eating, drinking, activity level, and any increased boniness. Despite my concerns, he was still his always loving, audience-pleasing self. He hung around my shoulders, eager to go everywhere I went. That is, when he wasn't already ensconced on my desk, trying to sleep on my computer keyboard as I typed or lounging on my papers as I tried to read.

In early September I saw a display and discussion of miniature roses on PBS's "Crockett's Victory Garden." I found them intriguing so I went to the Wellesley Library to learn more about them. No, Faust couldn't accompany me. The library was not *that* accommodating, even about my claim that he was an "emotional-support cat." His being a "service animal" wasn't an argument they bought.

It turned out that the miniatures are a breed apart from full-size rose bushes so you couldn't expect to find a mini version of "Mister Lincoln" or the "Peace Rose," for example. They tickled my fancy. I found myself desirous of having one … or two. I could plant them in big pots. If they did well, I'd inquire of the owners if I could plant some along the side foundation of the house or atop the rock ledge to cascade over it.

When my research located the headquarters for Nor'East Miniature Roses Inc., at 58 Hammond Street, Rowley, MA, in Essex County, just off Rt.1A, I was thrilled. I felt I had discovered a hidden treasure. As it turned out, Harmon and John Saville who owned Nor'east were one of the world's top hybridizers of miniatures.

The following Sunday Faust and I drove north, a short distance from the ocean, to see what they had to offer to the public. With the passenger's side window partially down, Faust stood on the passenger seat and inhaled the salt air. He gazed longingly out the window, and seemed to yearn for a walk along the beach. The one he had taken with me in Rockport, early on after his adoption and recovery, he had thoroughly enjoyed. He had chased the outgoing waves and run from the incoming ones. When he wasn't attempting backward flips on the wet sand, he was chasing sandpipers as they tried to probe for small invertebrates in the sand with their long, narrow, sensitive beaks. All until he became too winded to continue.

On the grass lawn, in front of the Saville's large greenhouse, there was an impressive display of many hundreds of plants in two-inch black plastic pots in holders on rough wood-plank tables. Up close it was obvious these were truly miniature roses, all were in bloom in a vast array of colors and petal configurations.

One, named "Minnie Pearl," had pink blossoms with a darker pink blush on the outer petals and a fruity-scent. "Iceberg" was a white climber with a slight greenish cast. "Red Cascade," also a climber, had dark red, velvety petals that would look smashing cascading over the rock ledge, especially in concert with "Iceberg." "Rainbow's End" was yellow with outer petals in deep pink.

But it was "Jennifer" that really impressed me. It was very fragrant with flat pink blossoms, pale yellow centers, and dark yellow stamens. The average diameter was two inches, a double, with seventeen-to-twenty-five petals. They were borne mostly as solitary, small clusters. Its tag said it was prolific, blooming in flushes throughout the season. That one clicked as a must-have. The colors of these different plants' flowers ranged from almost-fluorescent yellow to a brick/terracotta flower called "Teddy Bear." which was interesting, and definitely unique, but not all that appealing to me.

As I wandered by each plant, getting a whiff of its fragrance and examining the color palette and petal arrangement, Faust, who was on my shoulders, leaned down to get closer to the plants. Occasionally he swung his right paw in an attempt to grab their flowers to bring them up to his nose. But his front leg was too short to do it. I held "Jennifer" up to let him smell it, which he did for close to fifteen seconds, before trying to wrap his lips around it.

It was a warm sunny late summer day and the sun beating down on him seemed to be inducing lethargy. I'd brought water and his dish for him. He lapped and lapped. Once he was refreshed, I surveyed the vast array once more—just in case I'd missed something wonderful. So much to choose from. I wanted nearly all of them. But, finally, I bought "Jennifer," "Red Cascade," "Iceberg," and "Rainbow's End." They put them in a light cardboard box for me to protect them from potential ravaging cats. We returned home. I felt pleased with my exotic purchases. I saw myself as in the *in-group* of fanciers of mini-roses.

As soon as we arrived back home, I began debating where I could keep them safely out of Faust's oral reach. Maybe the living room mantlepiece since I wasn't using the fireplace. They would get plenty of sunshine there because of the three front-facing windows. As I arranged them, found saucers to go under them, and watered them, Faust crawled onto his favorite chair in my office and took a nap.

Two weeks later on a Sunday I thought I'd take us canoeing on the Charles River in Newton. It was Indian Summer, colorful and still warm enough. The canoe-rental shop is part of a fifty-seven-acre park which consists of forests, a meadow, gardens, and a marsh along the riverbank. From the boat dock you can enjoy twelve uninterrupted miles of the river, from Newton Upper Falls to Needham. Just for this occasion I had constructed a fabric-covered, split-wine-cork kitty lifejacket that I strapped onto him over his harness. It fit well and he hadn't seemed to mind its bulkiness when we were at the house. However, after I had rented the canoe, things changed.

No sooner had I pushed off onto the river than Faust spent all his time frantically trying to shove his right hind leg under the shoulder straps to slip out of his lifejacket. This activity was putting him in jeopardy of being bounced out of the canoe with his back foot stuck around his shoulders. In that position his head would likely have been forced underwater. With that going on and my attention distracted, any semblance of paddling, much less paddling in a straight line, was impossible. The canoe was slowly floating down the river sideways. We hadn't been out on the water for seven minutes before we had to return. I wrapped my legs around Faust in an effort to keep him stationary so I could maneuver us back. The moment he was on the dock he was fine again. What was going on? Was it the water's movement or the canoe or ...?

As I had removed his lifejacket and harness, I noticed his fur all over was beginning to look unkempt, almost greasy as it separated. I hadn't seen that before. Had he gotten wet in the canoe? No, I had checked that. And, surprisingly, mats were beginning to form on his hind quarters, making him look as if he were wearing jodhpurs. I thought I had been doing a good job with my combing and brushing him but apparently not frequently enough. As I puzzled about it, it slowly dawned on me that *he* was no longer grooming his formerly scrupulously clean, neat gray coat. Back in the car, now totally relaxed, he curled up on my lap. Once home, he nestled into his office chair and took a nap.

Two months whizzed by and lots of things were changing. I had become busier with writing weekly newspaper articles for the *Townsman;* sending out op-ed pieces to national and regional newspapers which were being published; occasionally having my articles in the *Boston Business Journal;* working on another book on different ways to promote oneself to get a job; giving seminars and speeches; and coaching. If only I had had a mentor to point out I was still charging way too little for the expertise, experience, and benefits I was providing, especially in my seminars and speeches. You can't have credibility if you don't charge enough. How can others value your services if you don't seem to value them yourself by not charging the appropriate fees? I guess I was still having difficulty seeing the value of all the resources I shared. Besides, that didn't help my bank account.

Things were changing for Faust as well. When I had walked him in the yard, he had always pulled me to the base of the old apple tree beneath the rock ledge. He couldn't wait to rivet his claws into the bark and scramble up the trunk, like a telephone linesman spiking a pole, to lounge on some upper crooked branch, slap at leaves, and stare down at me with a look of superiority. Now this seemed of less interest to him. Maybe the colder weather affected his ageing bones. Instead, he ambled along the grassy edge of the front walk, pausing frequently. When I let go of the leash, he eventually walked back to the front steps, climbed up, and lay down on the rough-cut hemp mat by the door. He was looking much older. I had considered taking him to Plymouth to take a glider flight with me but he seemed less interested in having any big adventures so I put it off.

A cat who was normally brimming with energy, despite his lingering lung problems, he wasn't playing as often or as vigorously with the string I dragged or spontaneously dancing, even when I put the "Blue Danube Waltz" on the stereo for him. If I stood up near him and circled my finger, he would get up and complete one circle before lying down. But his slumped body language suggested to me that he hoped I wouldn't request this performance again, or often. It was then I realized I had been observing over time numbers of tiny differences in his behavior, things I had not begun to put together until now.

He hadn't given me any indications he was in pain, although cats are good at hiding such things. I wanted it to be merely some behavioral phase he was going through but felt it was more likely that his age was creeping up on him. I never thought of his age. In fact, I thought his growing older would take longer. He was that feline paragon of interest, motivation, and joyous activity. His annual checkup wasn't due for another five months. As long as he was eating, drinking, eliminating, and seeming to enjoy himself, maybe I could wait until then. Well, I'd see how things went in the meantime.

Another two months rolled by. Christmas had been almost an afterthought with my schedule but I brought the Frazer fir pot inside for Faust and decorated the Monstera for me. I wrapped some empty boxes, in which I'd scattered dry catnip, for him to wedge himself into after he tore off the wrappings. I gave him a can of human salmon and a small red rubber ball with a jingle bell in it. Surprisingly, it grabbed his attention. He began swatting it around the floor. Some of the balsam branches I had again bought I set aside for Faust to roll in, which he did with libertine pleasure. The strong scent seemed to pep him up.

After the new year, however, Faust became fussy about eating. His salmon was still interesting to him but there seemed to be no longer any excitement about having it. I checked his mouth for plaque-covered or broken teeth or red, inflamed gums but didn't see any cause for concern. I had tried unsuccessfully to brush his teeth regularly. He didn't find that amusing. Oral problems were tough for animals and expensive for humans to take care of properly. Prevention was the key.

Maybe he was bored with is regular fare. I changed to a more expensive cat food, thinking he'd go wild about it. But it had a negligible effect. Up until that time he had always chowed down whatever I presented to him to eat. That is not to say he swallowed it whole, like a dog, but he ate a little at a time over a short period of time before polishing it off. He always finished it. Now, however, he showed only an intermittent interest in his canned food and dry crunchies.

Even when I decreased the amount of canned cat paté I gave him at each meal, in case it now was too much, food was being left in his dish. Since he eschewed his expensive cat food, I tried giving him teaspoonfuls of his previous-food preference, Friskies, multiple times a day. I hoped the smaller, more frequent feedings would make a difference, but it didn't. He was simply eating less. By the end of January, I could see his hip bones were becoming more sharply prominent. No question. He definitely was losing weight.

25

THE "L" WORD

Things were transitioning and not for the best. "Dammit, Faust," I said to him, "you're not supposed to get old." He just cocked his head to the right and gazed up at me, as if I were ignorant of how life works. He stood on his back legs perhaps to demonstrate he was still a spring chicken. I called Dr. Bridges anyway. His appointment was in two days.

When she examined him, she said his heart sounded okay and, of course, his lungs were still wheezy. His blood pressure was within normal range. I informed her there were no problems with his elimination that I had seen: No bloody stool, diarrhea, or straining. Dr. Bridges palpated his abdomen, frowned, then collected samples for a complete blood count, chemistry profile, urinalysis on him, and added an abdominal x-ray. I'd have the results in two days.

For those two days I kept him under observation: Everything he did and everything he didn't do that I thought he should. Poor thing. I know I made him uncomfortable, as I had when the blood chemistry tests, taken before we headed to Maine, erroneously showed that he had diabetes mellitus. I was anxiously pacing the floor in my mind until she phoned.

When she called, she said, "I have all his results." There was none of her usual upbeat tone. "He has high levels of creatinine, blood urea nitrogen (BUN), liver enzymes, calcium, and bilirubin. There is a finding of abnormally high lymphoblasts, immature white cells that are normally *within* the bone marrow. In addition, he is anemic and has protein in his urine."

I swallowed hard. "That … doesn't … sound … good," I stammered, my voice cracking with emotion.

"I'm afraid it's not. Because I thought I had felt something in his belly we did the x-ray. It showed enlarged visceral lymph nodes in his abdomen with thickening of the small intestine. And you said you haven't noticed any instances of vomiting, constipation, diarrhea, black stool, or bloody, mucous-y stool?"

"No, nothing like that." Oh, damn! She was about to drop the hammer. I was about to be told in no uncertain terms that he wasn't suffering from old age. Faust was in big trouble. I didn't want to hear it. But I couldn't put my fingers in my ears and la-la-la loudly enough to drown it out.

"Well, I'm sorry to say it looks like," she paused, "lymphoma, a cancer of the lymphocytes. They're a specific type of white blood cell. The lymphatic system transports life-sustaining substances and, normally, keeps harmful agents from circulating throughout the body. With lymphoma it will circulate these malignant white cells as well. But only thirty percent of cats have this alimentary lymphoma. We need to get a clearer picture so I recommend we do exploratory surgery. That will allow me to look around in his abdomen and take tissue specimens for biopsy to see more precisely what is going on."

My brain had stopped when she said the "L word." My heart plunged into my pelvic region. My legs felt heavy and weak. I had to sit down. This couldn't be happening. First Alix, now Faust? No. No. No. I didn't want to believe it. I wanted it to be old age.

As Dr. Bridges worked out scheduling for his surgery, Faust and I went to Lexington Gardens, one of his favorite destinations. In early February, only the indoor nursery was open. When he wasn't curled around my shoulders or in his knapsack, I carried him around in my arms, letting him catch the scent of the flowers in bloom and herbs he usually *loved* to sample. He had become a "regular customer"—of pots of catnip—so the management seemed to welcome him instead of making a to-do out of his presence.

Thankfully there had been no repetition of his first-time behavior there. While he had shown reserved olfactory interest in different flowers, as we had approached the catnip and herb table, he had jackknifed off my shoulders to try to land on top of them. His obvious aim was to inhale, lustfully chew, and roll in an induced altered state in this feline opiate. I had barely caught him in mid-air by his back legs as he still tried to use me as leverage to swing toward the display table. Then I had had to kneel on the concrete floor in the water draining from the just-watered pots to gain control of him.

If management had actually observed that *folie à deux*, I suspect they wouldn't have been quite so tolerant of him on his successive visits. But on this visit today his interest seemed to flag even when we approached the catnip table.

Looking over my shoulder for surveillance, I stealthily snitched a large leaf from lower on the main stalk of a multi-leafed plant to give to him. He only half-heartedly nasally embraced it and paused before carefully enveloping it. This was a cat who was always "Faster than a speeding bullet! More powerful than a locomotive! Able to leap tall buildings in a single bound" to obtain even a miniscule pinch of dry or living kitty "hashish"! I purchased that plant anyway for when he rallied and got his groove back.

On the way home we stopped at Friendly's to get him a small dish of vanilla ice cream. Instead of lapping it up, enjoying the milky cold tingling on his tongue, he let it melt in its dish. He sniffed it once and seemed interested but then apparently changed his mind. Maybe wintertime was too cold for ice cream for him. When we entered the house, I put the dish in the freezer just in case he reconsidered later.

On the following Thursday Faust would have his surgery. The night before I had to take away his food, as if he had been interested in it anyway, but left him his water. We had to be at the veterinary clinic the next morning by seven-thirty. When Faust stood at the side of my bed, looking up, but not jumping, I hoisted him up and placed him near my pillow. He slept with me, at my shoulder, but he declined to successively claim his other bed territories which had been his nightly ritual for years.

I didn't sleep immediately. My mind was scattered in a dozen worrisome directions. But I couldn't conjure up any positive thoughts. I'm usually a kitty can of salmon is half-full kind of person. Instead, I countered my pessimism by talking softly to him, telling him emphatically, "Mommy loves you and will make it better. You'll feel better soon. I promise," as I stroked his back and head. He snuggled in close to me and didn't move for the rest of the night. I felt like such a liar.

When I finally dozed off, I found myself back at Boston University in a building where I was supposed to teach a class but I couldn't find the classroom. I moved from room to room, then floor to floor. There was no one to tell me where I should go. Hours later when I found the classroom, I didn't have any of my materials with me for the class or Faust.

When the alarm clock awakened me with a start, the dream's anxiety was still lingering. I bathed and dressed quickly then placed Faust in his carrier without his general physical show of objection. "Aw, come on, Faust," I urged as my heart fluttered and tears formed, "how about a *little* fighting? Where's that kitty spunk you're so famous for?"

Carriers to him were not for fun activities. When he traveled anywhere with me it was on my shoulders, or, occasionally, in his knapsack. The only times he was ever held captive in a carrier was when he went to the vet or on a plane. This morning the carrier didn't exude the exciting energy of air travel where he would encounter all sorts of strange beings, sights, and smells, and where he could dazzle audiences with his performance magic in the aisle. Providentially, he liked Dr. Bridges and her techs, grabbing their faces with his claw-retracted paws when they placed him on the examination table. But he also associated being there with discomfort and unnecessary interruption of his important daily activities, like sleeping or licking his genitals—or what was left of them after neutering.

When I handed his plastic carrier over to Angie, one of the techs, unnecessarily reminding her to remind Dr. Bridges of his low-functioning lungs, Faust looked back at me through the wire door. I'll never forget the hint of betrayal that flickered in his amber eyes. Sadness cloaked his furry face. I hadn't told him what was going to happen. I had promised him I'd make it better. To him, I was certain, this didn't look like "better." I should have tried, though I didn't really know how, to explain it to him. But I didn't even try. I "assumed," I told myself, he wouldn't understand. I was not giving him the credit he deserved for assessing situations—situations involving himself. In reality I was thinking more about myself than about Faust. Publicly acknowledging what was going to be done and what it really, likely meant was not what I wanted to do. Deepdown, I childishly wanted to believe *if* I didn't say it aloud, it wasn't so.

He let out a gut-punching mohw that trailed off as he was carried into the surgical suite. I felt like a rat. And somehow knew I deserved it. His cry set the tone for the rest of my day until after four o'clock when I was to pick him up. I didn't do much work. I didn't want to do much work. Minutes dragged. Hours never passed. I couldn't sit still. I wanted to pace. I wanted to stuff my face with anything sweet, salty, or greasy I could lay my hands on: Krispy Kreme donuts, Lay's potato chips, or a deep-friend taco salad shell.

I told myself, "It's okay. Just because you're a psychologist doesn't mean you have to be 'professional, rational, and objective' all the time. You too have an inalienable human right to worry yourself sick, do stupid stuff, and imagine the worst." That unusual affirmation made me shake my head and emit a chuckle snort.

Seemingly days later, it was finally quarter to four and time. Anxiety and depression vied for pre-eminence. With a little morgue humor, I consoled myself that since I hadn't received a call telling me Faust had died on the table, he had probably survived surgery so I needed to go pick him up. That was *not* funny. Not in the least, I scolded myself. I left for the clinic trying to feel vaguely upbeat.

The clinic was glutted with concerned humans with their dogs and cats in varying stages of emergency. Some pets looked anxious, others curled themselves into fetal positions of quiet pain, some yowled. In general, they were being processed quickly according to their appointments. But real emergencies appeared and had to be triaged. It was controlled chaos.

And to think that at one time I'd considered becoming a veterinarian—long after I knew I wasn't going to go to med school to be a physician. But all it took was one evening helping a San Diego vet with a Borzoi that had had its throat torn open by some ferocious feral dogs to quash that idea. The semi-conscious wolfhound emitted a soul-strangling moan that clenched my heart. The wound was deep, ragged, and bloody, exposing muscles, tendons, and the dog's trachea. But it was the odor of the anesthesia that made my stomach turn. I became weak in the knees and began to black out. That was my ignominious defeat.

Despite his best efforts, the vet couldn't convince me my behavior was not only common but to be expected. "You're witnessing your first surgery and it's a particularly bloody one. Also, the smell of anesthesia makes everyone feel sick or faint at first. You'll get used to it."

But it didn't matter. I knew I associated too much with the maimed animal and its pain. I decided I couldn't be objective enough. I was sure learning, time, and experience would do nothing to make it better. I had expected myself to be stronger than everybody else in that new situation, and I wasn't. I felt like an abject failure. Thus, I sabotaged myself … again. As a result, regretfully, I never let myself explore this further in any way so I didn't know if that could have been a future possibility.

It was forty-five minutes before Dr. Bridges could take me into an exam room for a lengthy consultation. Initially she didn't look me in the eye. There she stated, "Examination of his abdominal area suggested he had patches of abnormal tissue everywhere." I clamped my lips shut tightly and pushed air down my throat to keep from letting a whimper escape. "I took tissue samples from a nodule on his liver—there was a mass of nodules there, from an enlarged lymph node, and from his small intestine for biopsy. We'll do histology of the tissue just to be sure, but it was pretty obvious what was going on. I didn't surgically remove anything because there was literally too much to remove … and there was no way of getting everything." She looked sadly at me. "Without any treatment, he'll have perhaps four-to-six weeks. But on prednisone alone he may have up to six months if the steroid is effective. I think chemo in his specific situation would likely just make him feel even worse for whatever time he has left with no real lasting benefit."

My lower lip began to quiver but I refused to cry. Up to six months on a daily pill? That was hopeful, wasn't it? Of course, that was assuming he'd let me pill him. I felt slightly buoyed up. Maybe we had more time together than I had thought.

She finished with a dispirited sigh, "As a result, I just sewed him back up. If he's up to it, you can do whatever will make him happy as long as it doesn't stress or over-tire him. Otherwise, just keep him warm, loved, and comfortable. I've placed a fentanyl patch on his back leg for pain which will last three days. If he needs more pain meds after the three days, we can apply another patch. But don't take it off yourself whether he needs another one or not. I'm required to do that. Keep in mind that even with the prednisone he may have only a month. You have to prepare yourself. It's hard to tell with GI lymphoma in cats."

She hugged me and I tried mightily to keep my deluge of tears from dripping onto the shoulder of her white coat. "By the way, just so you'll know what to expect today, because of his impaired lung function, it may take him a little while to exhale the anesthesia. But that will be okay and won't harm him. Just keep an eye on him. Don't let him walk around just yet. He'll be unsteady. It will take a while for him to get his sea legs again."

I nodded, my red face too contorted to speak. She wrinkled her brow, squeezed her eyes and lips together too, and gave me a thumbs-up sign before she quickly exited the room. She too had thought Faust was one of a kind after he had consented to display his plethora of talents for her one time in her examining room. I was gratified when she had applauded his skills with,

"Bravo!" When he finished, Faust had seemed to incandesce with marquee wattage, taking her response as the highest praise. I was surprised he didn't take a bow. That was something else he needed to learn.

26

STITCH IN TIME

Surprisingly, two days after the surgery Faust was moving around. I chortled to myself, "You can't keep a good man down." The black sutures on his shaved-naked abdomen almost ran the length of his torso. It reminded me of bodies that have been autopsied and sewn up except that his sutures didn't start with a "Y" incision from the shoulders meeting on his chest. I knew I must be wrong but he actually seemed peppier. How could that be? His tissue must have been very uncomfortable after having been cut open. Maybe the fentanyl was *really* good. Maybe I could use some of that too. After all, DuPont's slogan was "Better living through chemistry."

Since his regular cat foods no longer held any enticement for him, I made the ultimate sacrifice. I purchased a package of raw chicken breasts. Ugh. As a vegetarian, I didn't even want to smell, much less touch, the bird's dead flesh. But a kitty mom has to do what a kitty mom has to do. Faust's well-being had to take priority. Because he wouldn't take his prednisone as a pill, I was grinding each pill up and mixing it with a drop of chicken broth then syringing it into his mouth. That's not generally recommended since the steroid is so bitter. But whatever works.

I cooked a few small pieces with a small amount of rice. As I did, he sat on the kitchen floor beside me, looking up at the stove, waiting. The aroma alone seemed to stimulate his appetite. He pawed my ankle to hurry up. The moment his dish hit the floor he started nibbling his meal. He even licked the bowl when finished. Then, surprisingly, he looked up at me with great expectations as if to say, "Please, sir, I want some more." I gave him another tablespoon of it which apparently hit the spot. He lifted a paw to clean his long, white whiskers then sauntered into my office to lounge on his chair.

If he ever tired of cooked chicken, we could switch to raw. Since I was pussyfooting around the world of meats for Faust, I wondered about lamb. When humans' tummies weren't feeling up to snuff, they tended to be able to handle lamb well, especially with rice. I'd try to keep that in mind, even though the thought of slaughtered lambs was even worse than that of slaughtered chickens. In my youth my younger brother and I had had two lambs, Honey Lamb and Sugar Lamb, that we walked on clothesline leads. They died ostensibly because my father didn't continually move their tiny pen, as required, for fresh grass. Heartbreaking. Okay, maybe I was being a tad overly dramatic about killing animals for food, but still ...

As the days and weeks passed, I noticed Faust had shifted

from napping on the office chair to the radiator cover next to him. I assumed that was because of the heat. I moved the spider plants I had placed on it to the living room side table and snatched my dark brown wool coat sweater my mother had knitted for me from the closet. In the colder months I wore it a lot, especially in the house where I tried to keep the temperature at sixty-eight. I curled my favorite sweater into a kitty bed on the radiator. Faust always seemed to like the sweater with its large, dense rounded collar and leather-strap-woven buttons.

When I was wearing it, seated, but not paying enough attention to him, he always stole up to me, buried himself in the sweater to begin to gnaw on one of the buttons. Always the same button. Of course, the sweater smelled of me which I assumed was comforting, reassuring. Occasionally, I carefully washed it. I avoided having it dry cleaned because of what happened in my teens.

The happening was the result of a high school science fair project about nutrition I did with a mouse subject. I kept the mouse in a large wire cage on top of the refrigerator where it was safe from drafts and my cat, Sam. One afternoon after school when I went to clean the cage, I noticed the mouse was furiously scratching at patches of hair loss. Scabs and a few red spots dotted its back. Poor baby. How could that be? I regularly scrubbed the cage and the mouse didn't come in contact with the floor where Snoopy, our Pointer, lived. Locating a pair of yellow Playtex dish washing gloves, I gave the itchy little critter a sponge bath with tiny bit of shampoo, gently rinsing and drying it. But the next day its skin looked even worse.

It didn't look like an allergic reaction. Oh, crap! It looked like mange. Maybe it was demodectic mange caused by mites that lived on the hair follicles. Or maybe it was sarcoptic mange caused by tiny arthropods that burrowed into the skin. Whatever it was, I couldn't cure it with shampoo. My father stated he was not going to pay a veterinarian to try to cure the mouse if it could be done with one so small. Because mange could spread to our other animals and the rest of my family, I had to say good-bye to the mouse.

But I couldn't let it go into the wilds. It had been raised in a breeding— "manufacturing"—facility for the purpose of laboratory experimentation. It had never been taught how to survive on its own. Besides, it would continue to suffer from its rapidly-spreading condition as well as give the parasite to other animals. That meant I had to kill it and put it in the trash to be burned. But I didn't hurt animals, much less kill them or condone it *unless* it was to peacefully ease their suffering and there was absolutely no other way to do it.

Irrespective of my love of animals, I was expected to be brave, to steel myself, and act like an adult, doing what needed to be done. It was simple: My mouse, my problem, my solution. My heart twisting in my chest, I found an empty Quaker Oats cardboard cylindrical container in which I placed the suffering mouse. Tearfully apologizing for its condition and its euthanasia, I added a cotton ball I had dipped in the clear, slightly sweet-smelling cleaning fluid and replaced the container's cover. There didn't appear to be any other options open to me.

I had no idea how the carbon tetrachloride would dispatch the mouse but hoped it would be quick and painless. I knew that the chemical compound attacked the brain. In humans it caused signs of intoxication, headache, dizziness, and sleepiness. But even if the mouse serenely left this sphere of being, I knew I had killed it, purposely killed it. Ever since then, I've hated to have clothing dry cleaned because of the reminder. Moreover, to "protect" myself from residual fumes, whenever I *had* to have some apparel dry cleaned, I would obsessively air the garment for a week before using it. No matter what, I wasn't taking even the remotest chance with Faust.

To keep Faust from being disturbed and displaced from the office by my coaching clients, I had asked them individually if they would take their sessions by phone for the next several weeks or whatever was necessary. Some were reluctant but they all agreed, albeit somewhat grudgingly. In truth, some actually liked the idea of not having to travel to see me and asked to continue phone sessions. Over time more requested it too so most of my coaching was via telephone. To keep Faust from having to travel any distance when Nature called, I put his litter pan near the radiator and added his water as well as dry food bowl for snacking if he became desperate enough to eat it.

During the first week after his surgery, he began doing his acrobatics for me again. I didn't understand where the energy and motivation were coming from. Nothing positive had been done for him. When I had to change a bulb in the large, mirrored, modern light fixture in the dining room, I pulled the ladder from the kitchen pantry and climbed up. As I finished and was about to descend, there was Faust ... several steps up. I hadn't seen him on a ladder in years. And now ... after his surgery? But there he was: Eyes wide open and whiskers raised. His furry face seemed to broaden into a *grin*. I couldn't believe it. He seemed to be truly giving a full vampire-toothed smile. No question. I had to be hallucinating.

He stayed put so I awkwardly had to step around him to get down. What was this? Did he want to work on his performance and, perhaps, try something new? In that case, I went to the kitchen for some raw chicken encouragement. When I returned, I tapped the top of the ladder. Faust climbed up. I gave him a small sliver of chicken. He looked at me with anticipation. I said, "Down." He climbed down, face forward. I gave him another sliver. He looked at me, as if awaiting his next cue. "Roll over," I commanded and he did. A piece of chicken. I circled my hand and he did his Viennese waltz without music. Another tiny piece of chicken. This went on for nearly five minutes. Of course, he did not do his backflip or any of his splendiferous leaps on to the table or my shoulder because of his stitches.

By then he was tiring and the sticky chicken was losing its attractiveness. I carefully lifted him with my hand under his butt so as not to put stress on his stitches and placed him on his sweater bed on the office radiator. He languidly tongue-wiped the chicken remnants off his chin and his cheeks with a moistened paw, then curled in for an hour. Later he joined me when I told him the *Rockford Files* was on the television. We always watched it together, settled in the stuffed chair.

Miraculously his interest in performing his acrobatics went on for several days. At night after I placed him on the bed, he still nestled with me, staying by my shoulder, purring softly. However, he no longer took over my pillow, creating a fur nightcap for me, as he had in earlier days.

March was around the corner and things seemed normal again. He was eating, moving around, and seemed to enjoy going outside for short walks to take the air and feel the sun directly on his fur. I was allowing myself to be lulled into a false sense of security from which I was abruptly awakened when I had to run to the drugstore to refill a prescription. Thinking he might enjoy the trip, I put on a new royal blue sweater tube I had knitted for him to cover his naked abdomen, attached his harness, lashed him to my shoulders, and went to the basement to access the garage. But by the time we arrived at my car, Faust was restlessly shifting his position, making distressed sounds in his throat. Then when I lifted him off my shoulders to slip him into the car, he leapt out of my arms, trying to escape back into the basement. What was wrong?

When I caught him on the basement stairs, his ears were back, flat to his head and his pupils dilated. He looked frantic. Or was he in terrible pain? DAMN! I'd bet that my putting him on my shoulders hurt his abdomen. Feeling stupid and guilty, I took him back upstairs. After carefully removing his harness and sweater, I placed him on his sweater bed. As if I thought it would help, I apologized, "I'm so sorry. I thought you might like to go out on a little trip. I should have asked you first. Did I put pressure on your sutures? That must have hurt. Just lie here and relax. I'll be back soon."

He looked pained and confused, as if he were thinking, "How could my mom hurt and scare me like that?" He was still on the radiator when I returned. I kneeled next to him. He raised a paw toward me as if beckoning me closer. I leaned toward him and gently hugged him without moving him from his position on my sweater. He licked my ear. All was right with the world ... for the moment anyway. Apparently, he'd forgiven my temporary instance of human thoughtlessness.

In his second week he was sleeping more on the radiator than volunteering to dance around or climb ladders. His interest in performance seemed to be slowly evaporating. To make sure he was comfortable Dr. Bridges removed the old fentanyl patch and replaced it with a new one. She confided, "We have to keep him as pain free as possible for as long as possible. If he needs a third one, let me know."

Weeks were inching by since his surgery. We were still

going outside occasionally. Even though it was cold, when it wasn't too windy or snowing too heavily, we joined Nature for brief bouts. These outings would keep up for as long as he showed he enjoyed them. I'd open the front door and let him determine if he wanted to go out or not. When he walked toward it, I'd quickly slip on one of his sweaters and harness. The only problem was the wool of the sweater, under the harness, sometimes rubbed on the pinched skin created by his stitches. If he started to wiggle his body and kept it up, I would keep the walk short.

I entreated him to play inside and out. Surprisingly, one day he made an effort to tackle the clothesline I threw at him. It was not for long, but he had made the attempt and seemed to enjoy the momentary dare. He still pawed his small red rubber ball with a jingle bell inside around the living room. The only difference now was that he just ran more slowly to retrieve it.

Toward the end of March Faust's behaviors were changing more rapidly. Unlike most cats, Faust didn't hide, become reclusive, or isolated as his energy ebbed. He just slept more and was more parsimonious with his energy reserves. I know that in the wild they hide when they're ill to avoid predators. But I got a different vibe from Faust. Maybe that was because he had become an indoor cat. Despite conserving his energy by lying on the radiator, soaking up the sun's rays when it shone through the office windows, he was even more loving with me if that were possible.

He also seemed to be trying to please me in small ways. Surprisingly, he was still allowing me to give him his prednisone orally. Whenever he sat on my lap, he'd head bunt me and lick whatever part of my unclothed body he could reach. If skin wasn't available, he'd lick my clothing. That was not great either for my sweaters or for him as he, after the session, tried to extricate the wool fibers from his mouth. He slowly kneaded my tummy and arms, emitting a hardly noticeable purr. While those behaviors may have been soothing to him, he would look at me as if to ask if they were heartening to me as well. That he was still with me astounded me. Lymphoma was fickle as was the use of prednisone. I tried not to think about it.

His desire for chicken, whether cooked or raw, was beginning to fade. While he liked tuna juice, the tuna fish itself was too dry for him. Canned salmon, which had been his ultimate favorite treat in the past, no longer elicited his gourmet's interest. At Wellesley's Whole Foods at 442 Washington Street, I found a canned fish called "pilchard," which was flavored like tuna but moister. That tickled his palate a bit.

As we were closing in on the last vestiges of winter, Faust's skin was becoming looser as his cancer was burning his food up faster than he could use it to maintain his weight. His vertebrae shown more prominently like the points on thick barbed wire. The skin on his skull was becoming taut. Every once in a while, when he was encouraged, he stood up to do a half-circle. When he did, he always looked to me as if to say, "I've still got it, Mom." I'd scoop him up into my arms and lavish him with kisses and praise.

As he grew thinner, I ceased encouraging him to do any performance. I was at odds with myself about it though. Maybe he wanted me to ask so he could do it to please me. And maybe it would allow him to see he could still be the old Faust. But I didn't want him to feel bad or frustrated if he couldn't do it. I wanted his environment as positive as possible. Why couldn't he just speak English to tell me what he wanted me to do? I hated flying blind like that.

Unbelievably, Faust was still hanging on. There was no certainty about how long it would be but I wanted it all the same. Because of all the nodules and patches of malignant tissue she had found lurking, Dr. Bridges had pessimistically seen Faust as having only a month maximum left. But somehow, perhaps through sheer feline determination as well as prednisone, he had stayed around for additional time. He endured. But I knew that couldn't and wouldn't last. I was trying to prepare for that but emotional preparation was a myth.

27

PUPPY PADS

On an early April morning it snowed about an inch. Watching the flakes fluttering past the office windows, Faust showed interest in checking it out. I bundled him up and took him outside to catch the snowflakes that danced around his head and on his tongue. I dusted off an apple tree bough and placed him on his Wallendas's practice area. He rubbed his face against the bark, covering it with a stippled veil of glistening crystals. However, when the snow touched a spot of his bare skin below his sweater, he shivered. Before he could try to jump down, I placed him on the grass. He trotted toward the snow-free walkway, mohwing, seemingly claiming that had been good but it was enough.

Because Faust was still eating what little he ate in the kitchen, I purchased a medium-sized, circular piece of foam rubber which could have been used for making a throw pillow and covered it with a piece of dark blue chenille. This was to give him a second place to lie if he didn't feel like walking into the office. While Faust hadn't as yet had an accident on his sweater bed, as he grew weaker, I added puppy pads to his office chair, his sweater bed, his kitchen foam bed, and my bed … as a precaution. I had to keep him and his bedding clean and acceptable.

It was obvious from his litter pan that his urine was getting darker due to dehydration. He couldn't drink enough to dilute the toxins building up in his body. Besides, he didn't look as though he felt like drinking. He'd hang his head over his fresh water dish and just look at the liquid. Maybe he couldn't drink. When he would let me, I used an eye dropper to help keep his mouth moist.

At that time, as a veterinary client, I didn't have access to sub-cutaneous lactated ringer's solution to personally help replenish Faust's body fluids and balance his electrolytes at home. But given his shrunken body, the twenty-two-gauge needle under the skin between his emaciated shoulders might have been too painful to tolerate. Diarrhea was now becoming a fact of life and something over which he had no control. When he'd have an accident, his head would hang down in embarrassment and he wouldn't look at me. I felt so bad for him. Now when he wanted to cuddle with me on my lap, I had to place a puppy pad underneath him. He noticed my movement, paused as if feeling slightly insulted, but climbed on it anyway. All too soon he was no longer interested in my lap. I suspected it was not comfortable enough for all his sharp, jutting bones.

By the middle of April, Faust was staying in the kitchen mostly on his foam bed. He was no longer eating his pilchard. No pilchard, raw or cooked chicken, or tuna juice. I had even tried deli slices of roast beef, ham, and turkey. My so-called vegetarian kitchen had become a mini-butcher shop. No matter what he was offered, he turned his head away as if repulsed by the mere smell of it.

Whenever possible, I tried to get him to take an eyedropper of water, drop by drop. But soon he seemed to be having difficulty swallowing, occasionally choking on the miniscule amount of liquid. The panic in his eyes told me to stop that immediately. I wasn't helping. I was making it worse. Surprisingly, especially with his fibrotic lungs, his breathing hadn't become more rapid or noisy. Moreover, he didn't pant. I kept hoping that meant his respiratory system wasn't shutting down because that could spell his imminent end.

Zoologist Desmond Morris had stated that cats don't know about death or when they're dying. I asked myself how he could possibly know that. Faust may not have had or understood the bio-medical or philosophical concept of death but he surely indicated to me he was aware his body was ceasing to function properly and that he had to make the most of his time with me before it ceased totally.

As he lay quietly on his foam bed, I could smell his breath. It was bad. I couldn't tell if that was because of the built-up toxins in his body or his dry mouth ... or both. He was lying with his hind legs under him and his front paws ahead of him, not sleeping but with his eyes closed. He looked oddly serene and sphinx-like. Kneeling next to him on the linoleum floor, I put my hand on his front paw, caressing it. When I ran my finger between his toes and over his pads, I stopped. Oh, damn! His pads were cold. I clasped my heart. His body temperature was dropping.

As he lay there, his body was still but upright. No signs of confusion or disorientation. No obvious seizure activity. He wasn't restless or drooling or gasping. While the kitchen was warm, I wondered if I should place a hand towel over him as I continued to surround him with words of love and comfort and gentle petting.

What should I do now? Should I have him euthanized or just let him die here with me? Dr. Bridges never said she could make a house call to euthanize him. And I certainly wasn't going to stress him by taking him to her office. Even if she had provided such house services, I didn't know if that was what I wanted for him. Fortunately, I had be able to periodically get him fentanyl patches to help alleviate his discomfort. But, how do you decide on the perfect moment to bid him farewell? You certainly don't want to do it too soon … or, most definitely, not too late. I wanted his exit to be as peaceful, comfortable, and loving as was humanly possible. He deserved the best I could provide.

I assumed the time was very close so I hugged him and

kissed him and expressed all he had meant to me in our years together. Despite the tears and choked off words, I shared that I owed him so much for the love, happiness, and laughter he had given me, that he'd always be with me. I swore I'd never leave him. I promised he would not die feeling abandoned or panicked because he was left alone with some stranger who was about to lethally inject him. I was his mom forever and would put his final needs above mine.

My gut ached. I could hardly breathe. It was the most painful and heart-wrenching time I had ever experienced. I had promised him I'd make it all better. I hadn't. My love hadn't pulled off this supernatural phenomenon. To make myself feel better I'd promised something I couldn't deliver, not even for him. I felt so impotent.

Suddenly, as if struck by lightning, he jumped up from his bed! With this abrupt movement I fell back against the cabinets under the sink, my mouth open, gaping. He ran around the perimeter of the kitchen as if set on fire. In only seconds he was back beside me. He flopped forward onto his bed … and died.

In a state of total shock, I sat there staring at him. Involuntarily I moaned, "No, no!" Minutes clicked by. Then I picked up his limp, lifeless body and held him to me as I rocked back and forth. He had been my alter-ego, sometimes my evil twin, doing things I only wished I could do. He was willing to try almost anything, to explore, discover, and sample whatever life put before him. In many ways he had been my role model and life coach.

When I finally regained some composure, I took him and his kitchen kitty bed up to my bedroom. There I placed them on my bureau at the end of my bed. I covered his body with a hand towel as if to keep him warm. Even though I knew he had passed, I couldn't stop checking on him, feeling his rib cage for minimal signs of movement. My rational mind knew he was not coming back. There was no physical resurrection in his future. He had no future. But my emotional self didn't want to accept it and let go. Maybe there would be a cosmic tear in the time-space continuum such that he'd be revived, to jump on to my bed to nuzzle and sleep with me again … at least one last time.

However, when rigor mortis began to stiffen his limbs, I was forced to face, in no uncertain terms, that he was not coming back no matter how much I wished it. That part of my life was over. In a manner of speaking, I had to turn the page, begin again, alone. I had no choice. Even though I was left with the sweetest, funniest, and most delicious moments of his life indelibly etched in my memory, I felt abandoned, cheated, and deprived.

28

SAYING GOOD-BYE

The next morning with tissues in hand I located a small rectangular, heavy cardboard box that could accommodate his body. In it I placed a folded, soft hand towel on the bottom on which he would lie. I even rolled the end of the towel to form a pillow. His last catnip plant from Lexington Gardens had been thriving so I decorated the towel with its fresh leaves. I lay him on top on his left side, his head on the pillow, then crowned him with a spider plant pedicel, a stalk supporting flowers and baby plants he used to gnaw on. I set the small red ball with its enclosed a jingle bell between his front paws. I had only a small amount of my vintage Chanel No. 5 perfume left—a gift from an admirer in the 1960s—so I used my finger tip to place a dab on his head followed by a farewell kiss. My tears were dripping all over him. I blew my nose and left his kitty coffin on my bureau as I tried to figure out what to do with him.

I had to find the *perfect* spot. It had to have a view as well as be in tranquil, protected surroundings. It couldn't be at risk of someone inadvertently digging him up. I searched the house's grounds. Not the front. Maybe at the foot of his beloved apple tree. No. The ground was a mass of thick roots. The second tier of the lawn, back near the fence was available but not all that inviting. Besides there were tree and shrub roots all around. And neighborhood dogs, attracted by the smell of decay, might try to dig him up.

On the other side of the house near the back where someone had added on the half-bath and pantry was a slightly shady, open spot that overlooked the low New England rock wall on which he practiced. Behind it was a large forsythia. Its long, rough, gray-brown, arching boughs that cascaded gracefully over it would come into flower at the first sign of Spring. In a month or so it would make the area glow in the vibrant yellow of renewed life. That was good but it was not enough. He needed to be protected from digging animals. But even more important, there had to be a memorial for him and everything that he had meant to me.

I pulled myself together enough to drive to the nearest nursery. I couldn't go back to Lexington Gardens so soon. There were too many poignant memories there. Despite keeping my jaws clenched as I searched for the right living headstone, every so often droplets would slip down my cheeks. I did all I could to keep my face from squeezing itself into a red, crumpled torrent of tears.

It's funny that part of me desperately wanted to hide my

pain and another part of me wanted to share it with everyone, to dissipate it. It occurred to me that maybe cultures that ranted, raved, and wailed at a loved one's death had their fingers on the pulse of something inherently important to the human psyche.

It took me time to find *the* plant, a fragrant yellow azalea, to mark his resting place. The tag showed clusters of twenty-five funnel-shaped, light yellow flowers with long contrasting orange-red stamens. What was particularly nice was that it had thick, textured, elliptical green leaves which were considered "insect-proof." Furthermore, it not only closely matched the two plants against the back fence but also fitted nicely into this partial-sun spot I'd chosen along the foundation. The house owners could consider it a gift. They just wouldn't know how great a gift it was.

The still slightly-frozen, late April ground didn't yield as mercifully to my shovel as I would have wished. It took forty-five minutes to dig the appropriate depth and width hole. That accomplished, I added some potting soil and placed Faust's coffin gently into the space. I pretended to sing a little bit of an aria from "La Bohème," which I imagined he had serenaded me with as he walked the rim of my tub. I covered this more potting soil, the azalea root ball, and the remaining contents of the medium-size plastic bag of potting soil mixed with the dug soil.

This would be Faust's own TARDIS, to travel in time and

space like Dr. Who. I envisioned him as an effulgent spark of energy checking out the phenomenal Milky Way that we observed in Death Valley, and whatever else took his fancy. He had always been an adventurer. At the same time, he would continue to physically give back, nourishing the shrub as he had nourished me physically, spiritually, and emotionally.

I visited him daily, talking to him, sharing with him memories as well as what was going on in his absence. Over the years with him I had *finally* made a point to photograph him at home and away, being his crazy and loving self. But I had never taken the time to assemble the prints into an album. There had never been the need since he was always there with me. Now I felt compelled to sort through them and create that album. The undertaking obsessively held me. I poured over the many hundreds of photos, meticulously conjuring up his antics, the fun and sadness we had shared, and all the places we'd been together, especially where he'd touched other peoples' lives as well.

That took me weeks. Too often I had to stop and find something distracting to do instead. But once that was done, I could take my time choosing the perfect pictures to represent all the aspects of his personality and life for a large collage I wanted to hang on my wall. One day, well into the future, when I could deal with it better emotionally, I would also write his story so others could delight in it and share his brilliant contributions. Of course, it would be without his apt assistance. I put the collage on the back burner. First, I needed to peruse all the photos to remind myself that Faust wasn't a phantasm or figment of my fertile imagination. So many of our exploits had had an unreal quality about them in the ordinary scheme of things.

I had also purchased a camcorder to intermittently tape Faust's life, from his performances to his simply being the world's best cat. Thus, before he died, I had added his last acrobatic attempts to the videotape. The camera still loved him. He could have been a headliner with Cirque du Soleil. I viewed the tape and photos every day, smiling at his tricks and escapades and what had been a relationship for the ages.

While I had his life in images to behold and meditate upon every day, that seemed to take precedence. I kept telling myself there was plenty of time to create the collage later. Time was on my side, or so I thought. I would definitely get around to it one day. That became emblazoned on my brain as a prime example of my favorite expression, "Too soon old and too late smart."

Before I made the collage the unthinkable happened. When I moved from Wellesley years later, the moving company lost *the* box, that special box that contained his overflowing kitty album—ALL his kitty pictures—and the videotape. I was bereft. It was as if Faust had died a second time. I impressed upon the moving company its importance, that the box's contents were priceless. I didn't dare tell them what was so priceless to me because I didn't want them to throw up their hands, scoff, and dismiss the gravity of my loss.

They came up empty, stating they had "looked everywhere": In the truck that moved me and in the other household lots that occupied the truck over that long haul to Prescott, Arizona. They claimed they even "searched their warehouse." However, they never recovered it.

That was like an ice pick to my heart. If only I had kept them with me. If only I had put them in my suitcase—where they actually did *not* fit—instead of in a box. If only I had personally carried them. While the moving company financially "reimbursed" me for my legal loss, they never could compensate me for the actual loss with any amount of money.

29

LEGACY

But in the final analysis—in the harsh light of reality—I knew I didn't *really* need the album or tape. It has been said that nothing ever dies but only changes. That time itself does not pass but curves around us. And that the past and the future are linked together. Maybe that was true even in an unscientific sense as well. And maybe some truths are understood only in the heart instead of the brain. Faust had given me so much in so many ways he could never have comprehended that I could never ever forget any of it. It was soldered into the circuitry of my memory bank and occupied every cell of my being. Such as…

He had helped me recover from my social anxiety by showing me that taking risks wasn't so scary or dangerous.

He had shown me that trying to be "perfect" so no one could criticize me made no sense. That no matter what I did others would sometimes evaluate me negatively. It was purely subjective. And since I had no control over them, I might as well simply ignore their evaluations and rely upon my own, as he did.

He had shown me how the most seemingly insignificant things, like how a roadrunner runs eccentrically with prey in its mouth; what the first snowflakes of the season taste like; how a mountain lion sounds when it's seeking dinner; what salt crystals feel like on unshod feet; and what the ocean smells like on an autumn afternoon, could be interesting, fun, beautiful, and worthwhile.

He had done what he wanted to do, not what others, in general, expected of him. Of course, part of that was pleasing me and his adoring fan club. But he wasn't going to ask who would let him. If anything, it was a matter of seeing who would stop him. He was not about to obey all the rules. He was not about to change who he was, what he thought and felt, or his behavior in order to match anyone's *shoulds* for him.

He believed he could so he did. He persisted. His no-holds-barred sense of confidence and determination so impressed me that he had helped me to eliminate my ingrained sabotage tactics so I could finally demonstrate success. The success bred confidence. I might have been less likely to have written my clinical social anxiety researcher- and therapist-acclaimed book, *Diagonally-Parked in a Parallel Universe: Working Through Social Anxiety*, without his mentoring.

But most of all, without him I would never have known how one could love so deeply, non-judgmentally, and without hidden agendas AND be loved the same in return. His love was so pure and a special joy that only a non-human is capable of giving.

He had bestowed upon me a marvelous gift of hope, in seeing the hint of light even in the darkness, that I have since felt compelled to pay forward.

But still being so close to his death, I needed first to find ways to work through my feelings of loneliness.

About a month after Faust physically left, Spring made its appearance to wake up the world. The Earth was more angled toward the sun and the sun's rays were now nearly striking the equator from directly overhead. Warmer air was bringing hibernating insects, like bees and wasps, back into action, anticipating blossoms opening. Ice patches were thinning, becoming transparent, and riddled with tiny holes as the warmth defrosted the ground. Trees and shrubs were on the verge of budding, revealing their embryonic green leaves.

Purple, yellow, and white crocus were cheerfully crashing through the soil to compete with the masses of snowbells and grape hyacinth which reappeared everywhere to celebrate rebirth. Faust's azalea, to which he was wholeheartedly contributing, was readying itself to display its fragrant glory. Robins were pecking for earthworms in the broken ground's surface and grasshoppers among the new green sprigs poking through the dead brown grass mat that was the lawn.

I especially loved this time of year … as had Faust. It was

regeneration. It was a public proclamation. That in spite of everything harmful that humans had done to the environment, and were still doing to it, the planet was once again giving us a second chance. I felt it was reminding us of the incredible complexity and beauty of Nature that we enjoyed, that made all life, including ours, possible. It was the time of year that most sharply and philosophically reminded me of our right and responsibility to protect and save our one and only true Mother. Being once again on the verge of something new was exciting.

30

PAYING IT FORWARD

Staring longingly out the office windows, wishing with all my heart I were outside instead, I was going over my monthly business accounts, filing, and paying bills. Could things get any more mechanically boring that this? I asked myself. I had invoices and folders spread everywhere but on the radiator cover. Unconsciously I avoided that area. As I glanced at its now bare space, where my coat sweater had been so long before being washed and re-hung in the closet, I winced. None of that. We needed life in the room again. The spider plants ought to be returned to where they previously had sat. Fetching them from the living room, I lined them up in front of the office's three front windows. That made the room a little warmer and welcoming. It was more like Spring.

Suddenly I heard a piercing, repetitive noise outside. It appeared to come from the front stoop. Grimacing, I thought it was those damned dogs from next door … one more time. Their owner let his three hounds of some unknown breed out to run around the neighborhood, to ultimately whizz on my front door and dump on my lawn. I had spoken with him repeatedly but each time he swore it wasn't his dogs. Yeah, sure. Whenever I saw him, he patronizingly addressed me as "little girl." What a jerk!

If forbearance were a virtue, I should have been up for sainthood. It was a big irritation … but, I figured over time, that it was not enough of one to create a macho-male adversary by getting animal control or the police involved. Besides, he might well have been the type of person who would want to retaliate when provoked, especially by a female. I could always keep a camera handy to spot the dogs, although that seemed like a waste of my attention, time, and energy.

However, maybe if I could catch the dogs *in flagrante delicto* at this very moment, I could frighten them so badly they would never come back. But, as Faust would have opined, knowingly shaking his head, that was probably giving these canines too much cerebral credit. The annoyance wasn't only their taking such liberties. Their urine wasn't doing the varnish on the door's wood veneer any favors. You could see peeling and the veneer separating and bulging at the lower edge. Nor was it making the door mat an aromatic "thing of beauty and a joy forever." I'd have to be sure to replace it before the warmer weather let the stench of the heated, accumulating urine greet my clients. As the scratching continued, I was ready for them. Those ill-mannered, untrained dogs had taken their last piss at my expense.

Laughing evilly to myself, I rapidly pulled the door open. What? There were no dogs. Not on the stoop. Not in the yard. They couldn't have escaped that quickly, could they? Instead before me was a scrawny orange cat of indeterminate age, standing unsteadily on the door mat, swaying back and forth. It was apparently poised to continue to incise the door's surface with some archaic script. In a moment of wishful thinking I let myself think it was Faust in an orange cat suit teasing me to get my attention for a good back scratch.

This cat looked dirty and unkempt and had a large oozing, putrid wound on its neck. Someone or something had attacked this pathetic critter and left it to die. As I gazed back at the parallel tracks of undecipherable sentences it had etched on the door with its claws, it squeezed past me. It went straight for Faust's favorite office chair, weakly hopped on, and settled in.

My knee-jerk reaction was to display my displeasure. "Whoa, kiddo," I said somewhat brusquely. "That's Faust's chair!"

I stopped. No, it wasn't his chair any longer. Oh, damn! My eyes welled up. I was furious at myself for still being so weepy all the time. I cried every time I returned home and opened the kitchen door from the basement … and there was no one there to hop into my arms to greet me. Or when I turned around and thought I'd seen him disappear around the corner, wanting me to follow him. Or heard a piece of music he would dance to for me. Or sat on the stuffed chair in the dining room to watch 1940s black-and white movies, like his favorite, *Double Indemnity*. He had seemed fascinated by Barbara Stanwyck in her blonde wig and would stand in front of the TV screen to follow her every move. Or when I considered taking a bath, instead of a shower, but without his musical accompaniment. Or as I got into my car with no one there for company, to share even the smallest adventures, or to goad me to try something new or different. The strands of our lives were so integrally woven together that the passage of time could not break them apart.

Snatching a tissue from my jeans pocket, I wiped my eyes and blew my nose. At the rate I was going I was going to have permanently puffy eyes and a red, chafed nose. But now to the problem at hand. I knew there was no reason for me to be uncharitable to this cat, which was in obvious need, just because I still was grieving.

As I was having this dialogue with myself, the orange cat cocked his head to the right, as Faust used to do. I paused. "No," I thought, "don't go there. All cats do that." It looked me in the eye. It had deep amber eyes … that glinted like Faust's. I halted the incipient thought. "Come on," I whispered to myself, "Faust wasn't the only cat in the world to have glinting amber eyes." It reached out a paw and meowed, but it wasn't a meow. But it wasn't a mohw either. It was something suspended in between. I reminded myself, "So what!"

I knew I was being foolish. Because I wanted Faust back so

badly, I was trying, somehow, to make this cat into him. The fact was that Faust had died, period. He and his azalea were one now. I didn't believe in reincarnation. "What is more likely," I chuckled, "is that he'd left a sign outside for other homeless kitties, stating: 'A patsy lives here so look pathetic and she'll take you in.'"

I crouched down to the cat's level. I asked it, "Do you want to stay here?" It looked into my eyes. "Okay, that's settled. How about I get you a little food and then we go see the veterinarian to see about your infected neck?" It closed its eyes which I took as agreement.

As I stood and watched, the orange cat slithered down from the chair to the bare wood floor. Then it flopped onto its left side. "Oh my god!" I exclaimed, thinking it had collapsed. I pulled the cat-hair cover off the chair to wrap around the cat, to race it to the kitty ER. But before I could reach it, it shifted its bony shoulders and hips toward its right side, its hind legs pedaling in the air. Was it having a seizure? It didn't look like one. Before I could do anything, its legs dropped to the other side with its shoulders following. It wasn't having a seizure. Damn! It was rolling over!

"What the hell?" I mouthed, totally perplexed. What was that about? Was that for me? Then it stood up on all fours, ears forward, whiskers raised, its angular face looking very satisfied with itself.

That wishful, idiotic thought popped into my head again. I

chastised myself aloud, "No. No. No. This is not Faust, his spirit, or his doppelganger. This is just a kitty trying to get my attention. I don't need to pretend or conjure up an excuse to take in this cat. This cat needs medical assistance and a home." I pretended to slap my face back and forth with my hand and laughed, "Thanks, I needed that."

I had to admit now that there was no question that it felt indispensable to have some creature want and need me and be my constant companion. As I looked at its wasted body, maybe, just maybe, this cat was the one to fill that role. A warm glow crept up my face. Somehow, somewhere I knew Faust approved. He was still looking out for me.

The cat closely followed me into the kitchen where I fed *him* a tablespoon of canned Friskies. Yes, I'd secretly checked out his sex. After all, I couldn't keep interacting with the cat as an impersonalized "it." Friends-to-be don't do that to one another. When he finished his snack, and before he could begin his toilette, I opened up Faust's carrier for him. He eyeballed it, took the hint, and obligingly walked into it.

We left immediately for the vet where as an emergency his wound was cleaned, debrided, and temporarily bandaged. His fur was also given a spit and polish but required a little more bathing at another time. And joy of joys, he was given an industrial-strength antibiotic to take for ten days. That meant I was to have the questionable pleasure of trying to pill a cat … again. Trying to give Faust his de-worming pills was enough unsuccessful cat pilling to last a lifetime. The size of this horse pill made crushing it, mixing it with a little water or broth, and then using a syringe totally out of the question.

De-worming pills reminded me. It had started one morning bright and early after I had adopted Faust that I discovered he had internal parasites. On my dark blue bed spread were what looked like grains of white rice. What that meant didn't click until some of them began to writhe. "Oh my god!" I cried out, "That's tape worm!" After scooping them up in a tissue to drop into a plastic bag for the vet, I swung my bare feet over the edge of the bed. There beside my slippers was a wet spot on the wood floor. It looked as if it had pieces of string in it. What? Kneeling for a closer inspection, I discovered it was a pool of stomach juices in which half a dozen round worms gyrated. "Ooh, no! Faust barfed it up!" Parasites had him coming and going. He was obviously eating for three— disgusting. I couldn't get this addressed fast enough to suit me … and, I suspected, Faust as well.

As for my lack of success with Faust being pilled, before we moved from Sudbury to Wellesley, I was still occasionally finding previously-saliva-coated, partially macerated de-worming pills under the sofa. And as soon as this new cat was well, oh, boy-oh, boy, it would be de-worming time all over again. Until then, if it could only not shed its parasites in the house. Please! Had I really given this new living arrangement enough thought?

Back at the house when I released the cat from *his* carrier, he ambled into the living room. As if following a map, he drifted to the stairs where he unsteadily climbed to the second floor. Then down the hall he wended his way to my bedroom. There he awkwardly jumped onto my bed and curled up near my pillow. I think he was telling me, "You seem like a good enough human, even with the pills. Why not take you up on your adoption offer."

To seal the deal with him I had to give him a permanent ... and do it ASAP. At the vet where I had to give him a label, I said, "Just call him 'Orangekitty.'" I guess I shouldn't have sweated it because when I tested names on him, he made it perfectly clear by licking his nether region that he wasn't interested in some fancy schmancy literary-associated name. No, while it might have applied to "Faust," it wouldn't apply to him. He was a plain-spoken cat without pretentions. What you see is what you get—no more, no less. As a result, he was indicating he should be called something simple, fitting, and descriptive. To my amazement when I called him "Orangekitty," he put his paw on my arm and looked up at me.

And it didn't take long for him to let me know that he was a cat's cat, not some quasi-song-and-dance man. As such, he was *not* interested in considering an entertainment career. In case that had crossed my tiny human mind, I should forget it immediately.

While I mentally concurred, I still held out hope. Like

Faust, he was a touch-aholic with a turbo-jet purr. Even though I had agreed to do only what he wanted, whenever he did an acrobatic-like movement, I encouraged him to repeat it and do a little more toward the end behavior. Unlike Faust, however, he didn't. The most he would do, on his own, was roll over when he wanted a tummy rub and sit up with a lifted-whisker grin when we wanted his meal. It should be noted that he never waved his paw as if begging. Begging was no doubt beneath him. Although he grudgingly accepted a harness and leash, he disdained riding on my shoulders. It took me some time to fully recognize that he wasn't going to be a Gene Kelly or a Flying Wallenda like Faust. But ... then again ... why should he be? He was who he was, a very loving cat and a good companion. That was all that really mattered.

In retrospect, he reminded me of J. R. R. Tolkien's quotation from *The Fellowship of the Ring*, first volume of *The Lord of the Rings*:

"All that is gold does not glitter,
Not all those who wander are lost;
The old that is strong does not wither,
Deep roots are not reached by the frost."

Thanks, Faust, for *everything* ... including Orangekitty!

ABOUT THE AUTHOR

Signe A. Dayhoff, PhD, is a social psychologist with post-graduate training in counseling who received her doctorate from Boston University. For over 35 years she has been a cognitive-behaviorist, social-effectiveness coach, and author. She specializes in alleviating social anxiety, eliminating limiting beliefs, maximizing strengths and confidence, and overcoming obstacles.

An applied feline behaviorist and rescuer, she is currently kitty-mom to 11 senior, chronically ill, and disabled cats. She consults and gives presentations on improving human-cat relationships from both the human and cat's communication perspective and advocates for the adoption of homeless animals.

She has taught psychology at Boston University, University of Massachusetts, and Framingham State College and has done research at Massachusetts Institute of Technology, Scripps Clinic and Research Foundation, and Fairview State Hospital.

She is author of sixteen other books, 12 of which are self-help. Her other cat books include *Faust the Dancing Cat Tackles*

Strippers, Scammers and Bears; Remarkable Tales of Cats Who Whisper to Humans; How Intrepid the Disabled Kitten Triumphed to Help Others; What Faust the Dancing Cat Taught Me.

Be sure to check out her website at http://effectivenessplus.com